The Flemish Bond

East Anglia & The Netherlands
– Close & Ancient Neighbours

The Fish Auction at Great Yarmouth - George Vincent, 1828.
(Norwich Castle Museum and Art Gallery)

Published by
Groundnut Publishing

THE FLEMISH BOND

Published 2004 by Groundnut Publishing,
Gilray Road, Diss, Norfolk IP22 4EU

Text: Christopher Hanson-Smith

Editor: Ernest List

Typesetting and studio production: Eye Press Ltd

Printed and bound in Great Britain by
Eye Press Ltd, Diss, Norfolk.

ISBN 0-9527141-4-0

*Cover Illustration: Windpump, Flemish Gable in Norfolk UK,
Tulips, Honeysuckle, Paeonies and Roses in an Urn by Jans Frans van Dael
and a Dutch Seascape by Hollar Wenceslaus.*

CONTENTS

'The Flemish Bond'

ACKNOWLEDGEMENTS

There is nothing like some encouragement from friends to strengthen an author's determination to complete a project, and I must therefore record my gratitude to those who have given this invaluable support.

Derek Majer kindly put me in touch with Ernest List of Groundnut Publishing Norfolk who gallantly agreed to produce this book. William Woods, who runs the Dutch and Flemish Centre in Norwich, gave me the benefit of his great knowledge of the language and history of the Netherlands. Marÿka Hancock very kindly checked the references to the Dutch and their language. John and Diana Stanton gave much help over the chapter on agriculture, and also continual encouragement.

The Norwich City Council kindly allowed the use of the illustrations of the silver items in the City's Regalia.

The greatest support has come from Paul King, OBE, who not only read the MSS but afterwards introduced me to several of his very wide and influential circle of friends. His generous help in launching the book was also invaluable. One of his contacts was Robert Brooke, Chairman of the Anglo-Netherlands Society, who also read the MSS and then agreed to write the Foreword.

Finally I can but dedicate this book to Jennifer who valiantly kept me going throughout the years of research and writing.

FOREWORD

By **Robert Brooke** - *Chairman, The Anglo-Netherlands Society*

L ittle did I realise that I would enjoy reading so much Christopher Hanson-Smith's book "The Flemish Bond". It is a fascinating and easily digestible historical backdrop to much of our current understanding of the close links between the eastern counties and the Low Countries.

In the Introduction Christopher explains that the book "was written with the object of resurrecting those ancient bonds that bind the Netherlands to Britain". He has achieved his objective with an easy style, with great diligence and, clearly, much research. I found I was constantly reading on apace to discover more and more interesting and detailed descriptions. The title itself is an interesting play on words as can be read in the chapter on Architecture and Building.

The individual chapters bring to life the history, the events and the evolution of our close relationships as friends and neighbours – not always amicable.

Throughout the ages the rivalry has been intense, as it still is. This book provides a wonderful explanation of this aspect of our heritage as well as the agricultural, commercial and cultural characteristics that have shaped our communities over the centuries. Language and the origins of everyday expressions are explained and now have a better meaning.

Christopher's book has been a delight to read and fills an evident gap in our knowledge. It provides so much explanation and history. I recommend it for its enjoyment, its insight and its relevance to a better understanding into the links which bind us together.

Robert Brooke

INTRODUCTION

In 1954, an exhibition was mounted in the Castle Museum at Norwich to draw attention to the age-old links that have existed between the Netherlands, and the eastern counties of England. Included in the display was a true statement; that a visitor from East Anglia to the Netherlands is less a stranger than a friend. The first Queen Elizabeth well knew this when she declared;

"The Dutch are England's most ancient and familiar neighbours... the occasional wars are because each country wants to do the same things, in the same places; and at the same time".

This was as true in her reign as in the century to follow, when the two countries fought over maritime and trade supremacy during the three Anglo-Dutch wars.

However, in the last century, Great Britain and the Netherlands found common cause in the face of Nazi aggression. In 1945, when the Dutch faced deliberately imposed starvation, the American and British airmen flew hazardous, low-level missions from the many East Anglian bases, the bomb bays of their aircraft laden with vital food and supplies. Despite this help over 50,000 Dutch were starved to death.

The tending of the war graves in Holland is probably the most dedicated as anywhere in Europe, and every year children place a flower on each of the lovingly-tended graves of the paratroopers in the Arnhem-Oosterbeek war cemetery.

Geoffrey Chaucer, in the fourteenth century, knew of the strong trading links with the Netherlands as he included among his Pilgrims the Merchant who;

"with a forked berd in mottelee, and hye on horse he sat,

upon his head a Flaundrish (Flemish) bever hat"

Centuries later George Canning, the British Foreign Secretary, described with a pithy epigram the Dutch attitude to trade:-

"In matters of commerce the fault of the Dutch,
is giving too little and asking too much".

Until 1581, the present-day Holland, Belgium and Luxembourg were known as the Low Countries or 'Netherlands'. In that year, the seven northern provinces proclaimed their independence as the United Provinces, with Holland as the leading province. In 1648 Spain recognised the independence of the Dutch republic on the signing of the Treaty of Westphalia after the Thirty Years war and, under the guidance of the House of Orange-Nassau, the Republic reached its peak of prosperity – the Golden Age. Revolutionary France, in 1795, usurped Dutch independence, and in 1814 the former Spanish, later Austrian Netherlands, where most of the Flemish and Walloons lived, was finally reunited with its northern neighbours. In 1830, these southern provinces of the Netherlands broke away to become Belgium a year later, and Luxembourg in 1837.

Ever since Edward III invited Flemish weavers in 1331 to leave their native Flanders and help establish a cloth industry in England, the eastern counties have benefited from the wealth generated by wool and weaving. "It is the sheepe hath payed for all", declared a medieval trader in Norwich, a town that in the sixteenth century had nearly 4,000 Dutch, Flemish and Walloon immigrants out of a total population of 16,000. The Flemish pioneered the blending of other natural fibres, such as silk and flax, with the native wool to produce lighter fabrics that proved popular in the warmer countries of Europe.

These immigrants fled from religious persecution in the Netherlands both during Elizabeth I's reign, and during the next century's counter-reformation led by the catholic monarchs in Spain and France. These immigrants were known as refugees – from the French *refugiés* - and also as 'Strangers', again from the French *étrangers*. They arrived in Britain with little else than strong Protestant beliefs, and a wide range of valuable skills. They spread all over East Anglia, forming settlements within which they were able to worship and work in their customary manner.

The great majority of the Strangers settled down well, within two to three generations becoming assimilated with the local population by intermarriage. But they did meet hostility from those who feared that their own trades would suffer: workers in the weaving trade in particular. There was the case of a Norwich grocer, George Redman, who, during the reign of Elizabeth I, was involved in a plot to expel the Dutch and Walloon Strangers living in the city. He was found guilty and hanged; his valuable estates were then bestowed by the Queen on the Great Hospital, which was established beside the Cathedral in 1249.

There were others who, because they could not accept the Anglican liturgy, returned to the Netherlands. In the early seventeenth century over 3,000 Puritan Strangers, together with Englishmen who had married Dutch and Flemish women, left these shores. Among them were those who later became known as the Pilgrims; they first moved to Leiden via Amsterdam in 1609, and then finally set sail for New England eleven years later. One such Pilgrim was John Jenney, a brewery worker from Norwich, who was granted 'libertie to erect a mill for grinding and beating of corne upon brook at Plimoth' on landing in the promised land of America.

The theologian, Erasmus, came from Rotterdam to teach in Cambridge in 1510, and his reasonable interpretation of religion culminated in the adoption of the English Prayer Book of 1549, a landmark in the history of the English Reformation. A hundred years later Sir Thomas Browne, a physician who settled in Norwich, was writing his two masterful works – *'Religio Medici'* and *'Vulgar Errors'* – which established his reputation throughout the Netherlands, where he is now more revered than in his home county. Why else should there be found in Leiden a flourishing Sir Thomas Browne Society?

As space in the Netherlands is at a premium, it is always carefully measured and ordered. This meticulous attention to detail shows up in architecture, painting and even in the Dutch approach to football, a game they first learnt from the English. A Dutch coach of the national team recently told his players 'winning is not the most important thing... playing a good game is' – surely once a lesson taught to all true British sportsmen? In return, there is a strong probability that the Dutch gave to this country the game of golf, a word that derives from the Dutch *'kolf'*, meaning a club.

The quiet realism of the early Dutch and Flemish landscape paintings inspired not only the renowned East Anglian artists such as Gainsborough, Constable and Crome, but also the army of lesser painters who have portrayed the wide skies and far horizons common to both countries. The very word landscape is a corruption of the Dutch *'landschap'*.

The creation of space for human habitation is a great accomplishment of the Dutch and Flemish who have a saying '*Wien water aert, water keert*' which, loosely translated means, 'someone to whom water is second nature, controls water'. In a country where some polders, the reclaimed areas surrounded by dykes, are over four metres below sea level, the science, and practical application of hydraulic engineering is well understood. This expertise was harnessed to drain great tracts of fen in eastern England in the sixteenth and seventeenth centuries. Engineers from the Netherlands were active all round the east coast, from Canvey Island in Essex to King's Lynn and Boston beside the Wash.

The only part of the Norfolk Broads not formed by medieval peat digging, Horsey Mere, was created by Dutch skill, and following the devastating floods in 1938, the local farmers turned again to the Dutch experts on land reclamation who told them to 'lock up their ploughs for at least five years and only scrape the soil'.

Water, climate and restricted space were the elements that shaped the designs of the neat and formal pleasure gardens of the Netherlands in the seventeenth century; designs that can well be applied to gardens in the windswept eastern counties. The Dutch and Flemish have for centuries indulged in their love for cultivating flowers, fruit and vegetables. Clusius was a curator at the University of Leiden where, in 1590, he founded one of the first botanical gardens – the Hortus Botanicus. Through this garden were introduced into northern Europe the tulip, potato, tomato, and many other plants now commonly found in our gardens. William of Orange, the British monarch, displayed a Dutchman's typical passion for gardening, and part of his legacy are the majestic gardens of the Royal Palaces at Het Loo in Holland, and Hampton Court near London. His English Queen Mary had no less a love of gardening on a grand scale.

Today, Holland's agribusiness is 'number one' in Europe, and even the Pope, in his New Year's message, thanked the Netherlands for their flowers which give enjoyment to millions. A visitor to any garden centre will discover that most of the container-grown plants are imported from Holland and Belgium.

It was the Flemish, again with the aim of making the best use of their restricted farmland, who developed the four-course rotation of crops, a system later adopted by enlightened Norfolk landowners in order to increase the income from their estates. The Dutch and the Flemish introduced such invaluable cash crops as sugar beet, oilseed rape and hops, and continue to provide seed for the vegetable crops. The milk on supermarket shelves is most likely to have come from herds of contented Friesian-Holstein, black-and-white dairy cattle.

The wealth generated by the weaving industry, and improved farming practices, enabled the seventeenth century farmers and merchants to build bigger and better houses; these were often embellished by the distinctive, curvilinear gabling which is usually described as 'Dutch'. It is more accurate to call these brick gables 'Flemish', and then only if they are surmounted by a pediment. The interiors of these houses would boast such innovations as sash windows, vertical double-doors, built-in corner cupboards and metal bread ovens – all imports from the Netherlands. Delft tiles decorated the fireplaces: and on the iron cooking stove would have sat an earthenware frying pan – yet another Dutch import, as was the starch used for stiffening those fashionable ruffles and collars. And what would a Norfolk housewife do without her *dweil*, a floor cloth in Dutch?

But one curious fact is that, although East Anglia has enjoyed such a long and intimate connection with the Netherlands, the impact on the dialects of the region by the Dutch, the Flemish, and the French Huguenots has been minimal. An exception is the adoption of many Dutch nautical terms such as avast, boom, freebooter, yawl and clinker.

In the following chapters a more detailed account is given of what the eastern counties owe to the Netherlands in so many other and varied ways; whether it be in the house, the fields, the gardens, or the workplace. So much of what we take for granted in our way of living today can be traced back to the Strangers and the refugees.

This book was written with the object of resurrecting those ancient bonds that bind the Netherlands to Britain. An understanding of them will serve to strengthen that friendship which this country will surely need when facing the turbulence and challenges of an enlarged European Union.

A silk weaver working at her loom in c.1880.

THE PILGRIM FATHERS

No account of the ties that have bound the Netherlands and East Anglia together can afford to disregard the Puritans who became North America's Pilgrims in the seventeenth century. A common misconception is that all those who landed between 1620 and 1629 in New England sailed directly from English ports whereas many went via the Netherlands.

The Pilgrims who went first were Separatists who refused to conform to the Anglican Church and so decided to leave England. The majority came from Yorkshire, Nottinghamshire and Lincolnshire but many also lived in eastern towns from Norwich and Yarmouth in the north to Colchester and Canterbury further south. In particular, Puritan ideas had their greatest following at the University of Cambridge.

They made their first unsuccessful attempts to leave England in 1607, but towards the end of 1608 groups began to move to Amsterdam where they soon came up against the more militant Brownists, the most outspoken and quarrelsome of the Separatists. So they decided in 1609 to make a direct appeal to the Council of the city of Leiden to allow them to take up residence in that city and work in the fast-growing textile industry. A copy of this unusual request was entered in the Court Journal, thus allowing one hundred Englishmen led by John Robinson, a former minister of St Andrews in Norwich, to reside and work in Leiden.

Thus this document became the first deed by which the group which would later be famously known under the name of 'Pilgrims' was officially recognised. As such it is a unique document for the United States of America as well.

The Pilgrims remained in Leiden until 1620 and, although a

few had returned to England, the remainder decided to set sail in July of that year from Delfshaven to Southampton in the *Speedwell*, a ship of 60 tons which they had refitted. The *Mayflower* awaited them at Southampton and the two ships finally sailed for America on the 30th July (Old Calendar). The *Speedwell* sprung a serious leak 300 miles off Lands End so both ships returned to Plymouth via Falmouth. All but c.20 of the *Speedwell's* passengers transferred to the *Mayflower* which left Plymouth on September 6th 1620. (Old Calendar). Some of the Leiden Pilgrims followed on four other vessels between 1620 and 1629 but their leader, Pastor John Robinson, was blocked from coming to Plymouth by a strong Puritan majority among the merchant adventurers and died in Leiden in 1625.

Chapter I

ARCHITECTURE AND BUILDINGS

Mention the words 'Dutch influence' in the eastern counties and immediately there springs to mind the distinctive gabling that adorns many historic buildings in both town and country. Looking up at houses is so rewarding as that is the way to discern and enjoy their roof lines and fenestration. In Norfolk especially the curvilinear and stepped gables are very noticeable, styles that were first introduced by the immigrant Flemish and Dutch weavers and then adopted by the local builders. It was around the year 1675 that most of these 'Flemish' gables appeared.

Paintings of the Netherlands of that period show the tall, narrow buildings with steep pitched roofs and multi-tiered, ornate gabling that faced the canals. These houses were designed essentially for the towns where space was often at a premium and were not copied over here. Instead, there evolved from c.1560 a simpler style of curved, brick gabling that displayed elements of Italian, French and Flemish designs. This was because Flemish and Dutch architects such as Casper Vosbergh at Burghley House, Stamford, and Bernard Jansen at Audley End in Essex were working over here; and that Dutch textbooks were freely available for use by English surveyors and builders. It is known that Lyminge, a Norwich master builder who first worked on Hatfield House, and then at Blickling and Felbrigg Halls in his home county, used pattern books produced by Vredeman de Vries from Antwerp.

Inigo Jones, born in 1573 the son of a clothmaker, was sent to Italy to learn his profession as one of the first, true architects, and returned with many fresh and revolutionary ideas, most of which were inspired by Palladio. He was commissioned by the Whig politician and Norfolk landowner, Sir Roger Townshend, to help design a suitable country 'seat' on his estate and the result, Raynham Hall, completed in c.1632, is remarkable for the way in which the various European influences were so skilfully blended. The twin entrance lodges to the Hall have gables that are perfect examples of the Flemish and Italian styles.

One follower of Inigo Jones was the gifted architect, Sir Roger Pratt, whose greatest work was Coleshill House, in Berkshire, sadly now demolished. He also designed Clarendon House in Piccadilly. He retired to Ryston, near Downham Market, where, in 1672, he built for himself a country house in the contemporary Dutch style and surrounded it with formal, walled gardens. The house was later re-modelled by Sir John Soane and Salvin but a surviving oil painting by Danckerts at Ryston shows how the original building appeared.

Architects nowadays make a distinction between the true 'Raynham' gable that is surmounted by a classical pediment, and the 'shaped' gable with its geometric curves but no pediment, a style which evolved in East Anglia. Impressive examples of true, Flemish gabling are Christchurch Mansion in Ipswich, built in 1732 by a rich Huguenot merchant from London, and the 'White Hart' coaching inn at Scole, near Diss.

The simpler, shaped gables can be spotted all over Norfolk and Suffolk both in town and country. These gables were designed to be noticed and appeared on buildings whose owners wanted people to know that here lived someone who could well afford to follow the new building fashion. Others chose to build imposing entrance gates and lodges; today the same effect is achieved by parking an expensive car in the driveway.

As the persecution of the French and the Flemish protestants reached its climax with the revocation of the Edict of Nantes by Louis XIV in 1685, so Spain stepped up its campaign to subdue the Netherlands. The resultant flood of refugees to East Anglia and Kent generated further popularity for the domestic Flemish and Dutch architecture to which the refugees had been accustomed.

The Flemish gable was not confined to the eastern counties.

One of the first and finest examples of a curved gable can be seen at Trerice, a Cornish mansion, built in Tudor times by Sir John Arundell who had served as a soldier in the Netherlands. His Dutch architect had fled to this country in c.1572 following the earlier persecution of the protestants by the Spanish Duke of Alva. In the small coastal town of Topsham, just south of Exeter, several merchants' houses survive, their gabling financed by trade with the Netherlands. Also in Lincolnshire, in small villages such as Claypole, and in the town of Newark nearby, there are several, prominent Flemish gables.

In the old Hanse ports such as Great Yarmouth and King's Lynn the rich merchants who traded with the Netherlands adopted the gabling for their town houses. The dates of these houses can often be ascertained from the metal ties which were used to anchor the gables more securely to the roof structure. These are called 'anchors' after the Dutch word '*anker*' and are often in the shape of numerals that advertise the year of construction, or the initials of those who built the house. The earliest such date – 1578 – appears on a gable at Bracondale, just south of Norwich. An excellent collection of '*ankers*' from demolished houses can be seen at the Row 111 house preserved by English Heritage as a museum on the South Quay at Yarmouth.

The shaped gables are not only on the larger buildings; in villages there are cottages with outsize gabling and some smaller houses even sport a gable at only one end. The tradition of the curvilinear gable happily lives on in such modern, functional brick buildings as primary schools, council houses and even humble bus shelters.

Nobody has yet counted all the gabled buildings that survive in the region; Pevsner listed 160 in Norfolk alone but there are certainly many more to be found throughout the county. The majority of these are now listed as of Grade II importance and much valued by their present owners who cherish them as proof of the enduring links with the Low Countries.

The construction of gables with pediments and vigorous

brickwork required much skill on the part of the bricklayer whose art was revived by the Flemish and Dutch centuries after the demise of the Romans in Britain. From the fourth century onwards dwelling houses were built using wattle-and-daub, clay, and timber; only where stone could be quarried locally was it used to any extent. In the medieval period one of the first, major buildings to be constructed of brick was Caister Castle, near Yarmouth, where the owner, Sir John Fastolfe of Agincourt fame, employed Flemish craftsmen to do the work in 1432-36. They used the small, Flemish brick made from local brick earth, and it was about then that the word 'brick' replaced the older name 'waltyle'. Beeston Regis, on the north Norfolk coast, has buildings from this period with Flemish brick in their walls and there is a record of imported Flemish 'waltyles' being taken up the River Ouse to Ely in 1335.

Apart from flint, the only stone found in the region is the brown carr stone of west Norfolk although further west towards Stamford are the Barnack limestone quarries which have been worked since Roman times. For large buildings needing stone quoins and foundations the builder often preferred to import limestone from further afield such as Caen in Normandy, or Yorkshire.

Bricks, however, were the only durable and fire-proof alternative for lesser dwellings and fortunately good brick-earths appear throughout East Anglia, except on the chalk ridge that sweeps in a curve from just north of King's Lynn to the east of Cambridge. The shallow pits from which the earth and clay were 'borrowed' for local brick manufacture are in many places still recognisable as are the field names in which the borrow pits were dug.

A small, hard, yellow brick, known as a Dutch clinker, was imported into Norfolk from Holland towards the end of the seventeenth century. It served a dual purpose; to provide a useful ballast for sailing vessels, and a hard-wearing pavement for stables and courtyards.

The Flemish had their own way of laying bricks – the Flemish bond – which made use of more headers in the courses than did the traditional English bond. Often each course was made up from alternate headers and stretchers. This allowed for greater visual variety but resulted in a wall that was not structurally as strong as the traditional English bond. Lyminge was probably the first builder to use the imported bond in the walls of the outbuildings at Blickling Hall, completed in 1623. Three years later the new bond was used in the Dutch House, also known as Kew Palace, in Kew Gardens.

Bare, brick walls could be ornamented by the use of headers whose ends were vitrified by being dipped in sand before firing. The resultant metallic purple or black finish on the brick ends enabled the bricklayer to form geometrical, chequerboard, and diaper designs. Another innovation of Flemish origin was that of 'tumbling in' whereby short, diagonal, courses are laid at right angles to the slope of the gable to form ornamental triangles. Crow-stepped gables appeared at the same time as the Flemish gabling, and to protect the projections the builder had to use imported saddle-back coping bricks especially made by Dutch craftsmen until local manufacture was possible.

For centuries most of the dwelling houses in East Anglia were thatched with materials that came most easily to hand. In Norfolk this was reed which grew in every fen and still in much demand; however today some reed has to be imported from Holland or even further afield. Reed roofs, ridged with sedge and trapped between deep, brick gables and securely wired, can last for a hundred years although the sedge will have to be renewed two or three times during that period.

The main drawback with thatch is its flammability and when, in the seventeenth century, the first terracotta roof pantiles were imported from the Low Countries as ballast in the sailing ships, there immediately started a switch from thatch to the new pantiles. Oxburgh Hall in Norfolk, the moated mansion home of the Bedingfeld family since the time of Edward IV in the fifteenth century, was one of the first important buildings to be roofed with pantiles ordered especially from Holland. In 1636 Charles I granted a patent for the 'making of Pantiles or Flanders Tyles'; they were of a size slightly larger than the imported tiles. However, the black, glazed tiles which are so much a feature of the Norfolk farmhouse continued to be imported .

Pantiles, with their clever interlocking design, were traditionally laid on a layer of reeds coated with a mixture of lime mortar and animal hair – a *sarking* layer – to ensure a completely weatherproof cover.

The two well-preserved houses of former Dutch merchants in Great Yarmouth show how comfortable and well-furnished were the interiors. Scooped out of the walls are elegant, open cabinets on the shelves of which the owner would have displayed his prized collection of pottery while the deep fireplaces are lined with blue-and-white Delft tiles. The reception rooms are panelled in exotic woods imported from the East Indies, and all the windows have sliding sashes which first appeared in Britain in c.1680; very probably another innovation from the Netherlands. In the back quarters would have been a Dutch bread oven and the utensils so often depicted in the incomparable household scenes painted by the Netherlandish masters.

The fashion for coloured floor tiles, made in Antwerp, Bruges and Delft spread to Britain during the fourteenth century, and there was a brisk trade through east coast ports of imported Flemish tiles covered in yellow and dark green glazes. Recently discovered in Clifton House at King's Lynn were two pavements made from such tiles.

At King's Lynn also there is a building that is nearly a perfect copy of similar constructions as to be found in many Low Country ports. It is the Customs House, built by Henry Bell in 1683 as the Merchants Exchange, a copy of a typical Dutch weigh house. Sir John Turner, twice Mayor of Lynn and M.P, paid both for this building and the Dukes Head Hotel in Tuesday Market which Bell most probably built at the same time.

And finally, just to prove that the flow of ideas was not all one way, it is worth recording that the impressive Nieuwekerk in the centre of Amsterdam was largely the work of a master carpenter from Norwich whose father was a Flemish immigrant.

The floodlit south front of Blickling Hall in
Norfolk showing the curvilinear, shaped gabling.

The White Hart Inn at Scole, situated midway between Norwich and Ipswich, was built in
1655 with five, prominent, Flemish gables.

One of the entrance lodges at Raynham Hall,
completed in c.1650; an elegant example of a true
Flemish gable.

A simple cottage at Burgh-Next-Aylsham with a pair of outsize, shaped gables surmounted by
chimney stacks.

A typical shaped gable in Norfolk showing the date of its construction – 1683.

An elaborate *'anker'* incorporating the initials of the builder of the house in Great Yarmouth from which it was salvaged. *(English Heritage Collection)*

A perfect example of a shaped gable in the Cathedral Close, Norwich.

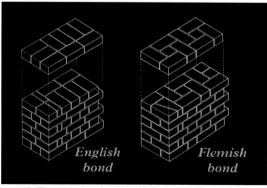

English bond

Flemish bond

A diagram showing the difference between the traditional English and imported Flemish bonds of brickwork.

An example of diaper brickwork on a 17th century Norfolk farmhouse.

Nieuwekerk in centre of Amsterdam. Largely the work of a master carpenter from Norwich.

A typical 17th century Dutch weigh house which was the
model for the Custom House in King's Lynn, built on the
Purfleet quay in 1683 by Henry Bell.

A modern bus shelter in a Norfolk village shows how present-day builders still use the traditional Flemish designs for gabling.

Another example of a modern building erected by a local housing association in Norfolk. The clever use of brick and flint embellished by shaped gables has resulted in a pleasing and traditional design.

The recently restored Customs House in King's Lynn which is now used as an information centre. The same architect was probably responsible for the Dukes Head hotel that overlooks the Tuesday Market.

An entrance lodge to the park at Felbrigg Hall, Norfolk.

25

Aldeburgh, in Suffolk, had strong trading links with the Netherlands and several handsome houses with shaped gables survive along the sea front.

Roger Pratt, knighted in 1668 for his part in rebuilding London after the Great Fire, inherited Ryston Hall, near Downham Market, and rebuilt the house in the Flemish style. The Hall was substantially altered by John Soane in c.1788. This painting by the Dutch artist Dankerts is of the original house.

Chapter II

WOOL AND THE WEAVERS

A visitor to East Anglia would be forgiven for thinking that the many and great medieval churches, whose towers and spires punctuate every horizon, were funded by the wealth generated by the surrounding fields of grain and root crops. In fact, these churches were paid for by merchants and landowners grown rich from the trade in wool, and the cloth woven from it. In 1612 there were no less than 1,201 parish churches in the county of Norfolk alone, and not many fewer in neighbouring Suffolk: symbols of the importance of sheep in the medieval rural economy.

The countryside, before the creation of enclosed fields, was effectively one vast sheepwalk with cultivated strips around the many villages. Shepherds grazed their great flocks on the stubble during the winter, and on the heaths and woodland pastures while the crops were growing. It was said that the best shepherd was a lame one – he could not then drive his sheep too hard and cause them to loose condition. Much of the wool produced was of poor quality, curly, and of a short staple length: ideal for knitted stockings and the coarser cloths. It was, however, favoured by Flemish weavers who blended it with the finer, long staple wool supplied by the sheep from beyond the Pyrenees.

England in the fourteenth century was the greatest producer of wool in Europe, and as exported wool was taxed, staple towns and ports were designated through which all of it had to be sold. This much simplified the collection of tax on which the monarchy depended. Antwerp was for many years the foremost continental staple port until 1353 when Edward III, who had married the Flemish princess, Philippa of Hainault, decreed that Calais should become the main trading centre for wool. The other staples were

Norwich, Ipswich, King's Lynn and Great Yarmouth.

During Edward's reign a Flemish weaver, John Kempe, settled in Norfolk, and encouragement was given to his wife's kinsmen to settle in the eastern counties. These Flemish immigrants were attracted to the valleys of rivers such as the Stour, Colne, and Orwell where they could rely on plentiful supplies of clean water required for the fulling and scouring of the woven cloth. In Norfolk, where there are fewer rivers, the weavers concentrated on producing a worsted cloth that did not need to be fulled.

In the highly trained, professional armies of Edward, the knights and their followers returned from the Crusades with a taste for the exotic and bright fabrics favoured by the Saracens, and expected the skilful Flemish weavers to create a matching range.

When, in 1336, Philip VI of France had the English wool merchants arrested, Edward III retaliated by stopping all wool exports to the Netherlands; this dispute over wool triggered the start of the devastating Hundred Years War. The Flemish burghers and weavers turned to England for support and, finding there a cautious welcome, began to use a mixture of local wools and yarns for the production of the 'new draperies', which were welcomed in the export markets, especially those with warmer climates.

Cloth quality was strictly controlled by the gilds, or guilds, which were craft or trade societies with a strong, religious element. The term 'guild' derives from the Saxon word *gildan* – 'to pay'; the members paid towards the costs of the brotherhood, and, as they wore a distinctive costume or livery, the guilds became known as livery companies. These guilds had particularly strong support in the weaving communities of Essex and Suffolk. The Fullers guild was incorporated as a company in 1480: the Clothworkers were then established by Royal Charter in 1528.

Exports reached their peak at the end of the fifteenth century with Ipswich, Lynn, and Yarmouth sharing the lucrative trade with London, Boston, and Hull. Cloth was sent as far afield as Russia, where the Cossacks liked the English fabrics, and even Turkey. Lavenham, in Suffolk, was famous for its 'blue' broadcloth, while

Sudbury, where the Flemish had long been active, became the main supplier of cloth in Suffolk. Essex weavers concentrated on the famous 'whites' – cloth that was first fulled, and then stretched to dry on tenter hooks, set in wooden frames.

In the Essex village of Coggeshall is Paycockes, an early sixteenth century house, rich in carved woodwork, and now in the care of the National Trust. It was here that an Italian, having arrived via the Netherlands, first taught the art of spinning wool with a distaff. The spun yarn was then woven into Coxall cloth, later known as Coggeshall 'white'. One hundred years later there were working looms in Paycockes producing a 'bay' – a fine twill with a long nap.

The religious upheaval of the Reformation was to have a profound effect on the weaving industry in East Anglia. In 1517, Martin Luther nailed his ninety five religious theses to the church door of the tower at Wittenburg where he was a monk, and seventeen years later John Calvin was expelled from his native France for spreading the new Protestant faith. By 1521 Lutheran tracts were circulating in Norfolk, and Henry VIII was pursuing his doctrine of non-Papal Catholicism. It was his son, Edward VI, under the influence of the Regent Somerset, who wholeheartedly supported the moderate Protestantism, and allowed the establishment of the first 'foreign' churches in England for the immigrant French and Dutch refugees.

As the Reformation swept through Europe, Philip II, who led the counter-Reformation movement from his bleak monastery at Escorial outside Madrid, ordered the Duke of Alva to impose Catholicism by force on the Netherlands. Antwerp was ravaged, and his ruthless campaign unleashed a flood of frightened Protestants, many of whom fled to south-east England via Holland. They brought with them little but their skills and austere religious beliefs. The many weavers amongst them proceeded to disperse, and settle in small, 'Stranger' communities in the eastern counties. They soon demonstrated their ability to create the refined and lighter draperies that were marketed under such exotic names as perpetuana, mockadoe and frizado. The Flemish were also skilled at dyeing fabrics, and introduced such popular shades as 'popinjay green', and 'turtle and willow' – which proves that not much has changed in the fashion scene over the years. The expression 'dyed in the wool' was first heard at this time; the theatre building now known as the Maddermarket in Norwich was built on the site of the market where the various dyes were sold.

Overall, non-conformity became synonymous with cloth-making, as Puritan values were dominant among the Strangers and so, in 1565, the Mayor and Corporation of Norwich took advantage of the exodus of persecuted weavers from the Netherlands. With the help of the Elders of the Dutch church, twenty four Dutch and six Walloon master craftsmen were invited, with their households, to settle in the city. The Duke of Norfolk assisted by obtaining a Royal licence that allowed these Strangers to exercise their traditional trade of making 'bays, arras, sayes, tapestry, mockadoes, and other such outlandish commodities as hath not been used to be made within our realme of England'.

Many other Strangers followed until, in 1582, they comprised one third of the population of Norwich: a fine example of '*corpus corporaticum et ponticum*'. Mild controls ensured that immigrants were able to settle happily, and worship how they pleased. They were granted the church of St Mary-the-Less, in Queen Street, as their cloth hall, and this later became a place of worship for the French-speaking Walloons, with services conducted in French. Because of a dispute within the established church in Norwich from 1565 until 1637, the Walloons were granted the use of the Bishop's chapel.

The Dutch and Flemish were given the chapel of Blackfriars, originally the choir of the Dominican friary of St Andrews, next door. In 1570, Norwich was described as 'a godly city', thanks to the presence of so many devout Strangers, and, as a further example of a caring community, a fund was established to help the poor and pay for the education of their children.

The floor of the Blackfriars church was once dotted with memorials, in Dutch, to deceased members of the Strangers' community, but today only one brass remains, to the memory of Theophilus Ellison, pastor to the church from 1639, whose achievements are summarised in Dutch, Latin, and English on adjacent plaques. They read "Here lyeth the body of Mr Theophilus Ellison who having been borne in this Citty, Anno 1609, After succeeded his Father in the Pastorall Office to the Dutch Congregation, wherein as his father before him, hee faithfully served God 36 years, and died June 1st 1676.

Doe not beleeve that Ellison is dead.

His dust lyes here his soule to heaven fled".

Theophilus's father, Johannes, married into the Dutch community in Norwich and was sent to Leiden for training as a pastor. He and his wife were friendly with Rembrandt in Leiden where, in 1634, he painted separate portraits of them, and these now hang in the Museum of Fine Arts in Boston, USA.

Colchester also had a long-standing community of Strangers, and their leader, in 1549, was a master weaver called Giles Tayspill. Between 1565 and 1571, as in Norwich, there was a large influx of exiled weavers from the Netherlands, whose specialities were bays and says. Their finished cloth had to be examined in the Dutch Bay Hall, where metal seals were affixed as a guarantee of quality. The Colchester bays were much sought after in Europe, and were exchanged for linen, beer, cheese, and pottery. Today, the Fire Office in the High Street stands on the site of the old Bay Hall but examples of the seals, and a bolt of original bay cloth, can be seen in the Castle Museum. The Strangers lived in the Dutch quarter in which many of their colourful houses still overlook the narrow streets and alleyways.

During the Civil War, in 1648, Colchester was besieged and taken by General Fairfax; he imposed a punitive fine of £12,000 on the townspeople and half of this great sum had to be found by the long-suffering Stranger community. This unfair levy was a symbol of the envy and distrust that was often shown by the poorer folk towards the Strangers, whose industry and austere way of life were in marked contrast to their own. The congregation of the Dutch church in Colchester was closely allied to the Austin Friars church in London, the acknowledged centre for Dutch and Flemish immigrants in the metropolis.

The Revocation of the Edict of Nantes by Louis XIV in 1685, unleashed a massive exodus of French Huguenot refugees who found a ready welcome among the Stranger communities already settled in London and the south-east. Many of the weavers amongst them moved to Colchester where water from the river Colne was found to be ideal for the production of the new fabrics. They were not welcomed everywhere, however, and those who tried to settle at Halstead were soon driven out by local weavers, fearful of losing their jobs to the industrious newcomers.

The main centres of weaving were kept supplied with yarn that was spun as a cottage industry throughout the region, giving employment to many women and their children. The word 'spinster' derives from the poorer, single women who were dependent on spinning for a living.

By 1630 it was estimated that half the working population of Essex was engaged in the cloth industry, and similar occupations such as lace-making, ribbon-weaving, and the knitting of hose in a wide range of colours. An observer in Norwich, in 1690, reckoned that over half the freemen were engaged in the textile trade, while most of the women were knitting thousands of pairs of stockings and hose, most of which were for export.

By the end of the sixteenth century, the markets for the traditional and heavier woollen cloths had much diminished, and the places that depended upon their manufacture either had to adapt to the new, imported techniques, or simply become suppliers of yarn. This happened at Lavenham, in Suffolk, where the superb church and medieval half-timbered buildings, are a reminder of the town's earlier importance and its steady decline thereafter.

Large villages such as Finchingfield, in Essex, relied on the spinning of yarn, as did Bocking, where much later the Courtauld family, whose great grandparents were Huguenot silversmiths in London, established their silk weaving mill. Hedingham was settled by the Dutch in the sixteenth century, and bays continued to be woven there for well over 300 years. It was a similar story at Bourne, on the outskirts of Colchester, where a party of Dutch immigrants took over the redundant watermill, built in 1591 with flamboyant gables which were no doubt designed by earlier Flemish exiles. Here the Dutch wove white bay, and dried the cloth on tenterhooks in the meadows beside the small stream that still runs beneath the mill. As this cloth later became coarser and dyed green, it was known as baize. By 1826, the only places in Essex where baize was still woven were at Bourne Mill and at Bocking: by 1840 both mills had shut down.

'Say' was a thicker cloth, more like modern serge, and much in demand for aprons and bed hangings. Ironically, a major export outlet for say was in the Catholic countries in Europe, where the monks and nuns much favoured it – a cloth woven by Protestant refugees from Catholic persecution. The many portraits of monks by the great Spanish artist, Zurbaran, show their flowing white habits in luminous detail.

To achieve the great variety of cloth demanded by the new fashions, the weavers used other natural fibres to blend with the wool. Silk appeared in many fabrics such as the black bombazine, much favoured by women in mourning. In the courtyard of the present Walloon church in Norwich, there grows a healthy mulberry tree, planted to commemorate the cultivation of silkworms which fed on the mulberry leaves.

A linen warp, with a worsted weft, produced a cloth popular for bed covers: this was called 'tiretaine' by the Walloon weavers, a name that became the Flemish 'turtein', and then 'tartan' in English. Cotton became increasingly popular and the hard-wearing cloth now known as denim originated in the French town of Nîmes.

Worsted cloth was, however, the mainstay of the weaving industry since the advent of the Flemings, especially in Norfolk, where the village of Worstead is reputed to have given its name to the smooth cloth woven from yarn spun from long-stapled wool, and then combed to lay the fibres parallel. The Cotswold breed of sheep provided the ideal fleece for worsted production as it could be blended with the coarser wool of lesser breeds of sheep before they were so successfully improved by Lord Coke of Norfolk. The weavers also imported wool of the Merino-type sheep traditionally reared in Spain. The finest worsted cloth was known as camlet, and Norwich became the centre of production which, as it expanded, was controlled by an ever-growing complexity of rules. These irked many of the weavers, who preferred to live and work in the surrounding small towns. Weaving thus became a true cottage industry, and the surviving houses of the weavers can often be spotted by their large windows, and half-timbered construction, akin to so many old dwellings in the Netherlands.

To revive the spirits of the weavers during the tedious hours at the looms, the Flemish brought with them their canaries which could sing the day through. Today, the Norfolk canary with its bright, yellow plumage is considered by fanciers as the best, and has even given its name to the Norwich City football club whose training ground was once the site of the canary aviaries. The Club's players sport the distinctive yellow and green 'strip', and call themselves Canaries.

The industrial revolution, and imported cotton, sounded the death knell for the traditional weaving industry; by 1770 the West Riding of Yorkshire had overtaken Norfolk as the main producer of worsted cloth. Despite the early, revolutionary inventions of power-driven machinery for making cotton fabric, the technical problems involved in preparing wool for weaving were not wholly overcome until the mid-nineteenth century. The combing of the wool by machine presented the greatest difficulties, and it seemed as if the spirits of all the Dutch and Flemish weavers of past centuries had united to delay the final demise of an industry that had generated so much wealth and prestige for the eastern counties of England.

Bourne Mill, Colchester – built 1591. The arabesque gables are the earliest example of the Dutch style to be found in Essex.

The canaries that were to be found in nearly all the weaving lofts.

The garden of the Guildhall at Lavenham in Suffolk, where are grown plants from which the traditional dyes were obtained.

A typical weaver's loom as used throughout the 14th and 15th centuries.

The Old Bedford River at Earith, cut in 1636-37.

The New Bedford River washes at Welney.

The windpump at Wicken Fen.

A Lowestoft china jug, decorated with the painting of a
Dutch post mill.

Chapter III

WATER - FRESH AND FLOWING

"The making of new land belongs to God alone for He
gives to some people the wit and the strength to do it"

The creation of the Netherlands was driven by the need of the
early inhabitants to survive on the patches of dry land cradled
within the deltas of three great rivers – the Rhine, the Maas, and the
Schelde. Floods continually menaced these precarious settlements in a
country of which 40% lay below sea level. History relates how, in
1287, 50,000 people drowned in a raging flood and since then there
has been serious flooding on at least 140 occasions. The St
Elizabeth's Day flood of November, 1421, when 500 hectares were
inundated, was for long regarded as a just retribution for a people
who had lived in sin and a catastrophe that rivalled the later ravages
of the Black Death. In more recent times the 1953 inundation
caused much greater havoc in Holland than in East Anglia; 1,800
people died and 152,000 hectares of hard-won farmland were
swamped by the sea.

For ninety years the struggle for independence from Spain
coincided with an intensive battle to preserve the reclaimed land and
to extend it. In 1574 the United Provinces had to face the supreme
test when the town of Leiden was invested by the Spanish forces.
The defence of the town was in the hands of an armed militia as
there were no regular troops available to fight. William of Orange
decided upon a drastic plan of inundation as the only way of saving
Leiden; the sluices were opened up, the dykes breached. The Spanish
awoke to find their encampments threatened by rising waters, and
fighting vessels under full sail bearing down upon them over open
water where days before there had been dry land. For the Dutch
this deliverance from their hated enemies was a sure sign that God –

a Protestant God – was on their side.

The Dutch have responded to the constant threat of the sea by building dykes to keep out the salt water and then allowing the fresh river waters to flood reclaimed land, known as polders. The term used to 'inn' or reclaim land derives from the Dutch word *'inpolderen'*. Canals became vital channels of communication and trade between the towns and ports. Not surprising therefore that Dutch hydraulic engineers have for centuries been much in demand by other countries with similar problems of encroaching seas and flood control. In East Anglia these specialists became active in the sixteenth century and one of the first was a certain Peter Peterson whose task as dyke reeve was to supervise the sea defences at Haddiscoe, near Lowestoft. A memorial tablet to his wife, dated 1525 and inscribed in Dutch, is set into the floor of the aisle of Haddiscoe church.

One of the first land reclamation projects on the east coast was undertaken between 1618 and 1621 at Canvey Island in Essex. The Dutchman, Joas van Croppenburg, was the engineer who undertook to drain 3,600 acres (1,460 hectares) of marsh in return for one third of the reclaimed lands. This form of payment was adopted in response to the experience of Cornelius Vermuyden at Dagenham in Essex where he had undertaken drainage work. He had soon realised that, with land in hand or promised, an engineer's credit was good for borrowing money to cover stage payments to men and for materials. As reminders of the Dutch and Flemish occupation of the island are two thatched, octagonal brick cottages, one of which houses a Dutch Cottage museum.

Up the coast at Great Yarmouth another Dutchman, Joas Janssen, was commissioned to dredge the harbour mouth so as to make it navigable, and further round the Norfolk coast at Wells-next-the-Sea, the surrounding marshes were drained by Freeston, a Flemish engineer. At Salthouse nearby, where the shingle bank was broached by the 1953 storm and the marshes flooded, the Dutchman Jan van Hasedunk built the first protective embankment in 1637.

However it was around the Wash that the drainage skills of the Dutch and Flemish were in greatest need. The Romans were the first to attempt to drain part of this great malarial-ridden swamp that covered over 2,000 square miles (5,200 square km) and some of their dykes can still be traced. Part of this waste was known as the Great Level, c.680,000 acres (273,000 hectares) of a peaty top soil lying on blue clay and submerged most of the year. In 1607 the fens south of the river Nene, that runs through Peterborough, suffered from a disastrous flood which drowned many of the inhabitants and their livestock. This catastrophe persuaded James I to appoint Justice Popham as a Commissioner with a brief to survey the region and recommend how future floods might be avoided and valuable farmland created.

The first attempt to drain c.37,000 acres (15,000 hectares), financed by a hopeful band of London merchants, was a failure. The King, nothing daunted, turned his attention to the Royal Chase at Hatfield, near Doncaster, which included the Island of Axholme. Knowing how experienced the Dutch were at land reclamation, he invited two engineers to tender for the work; they were Jan Berents Westerdyke and Cornelius Vermuyden. The latter, from Maartensdijk in Zeeland, won the contract to drain the great marsh of c.70,000 acres (28,000 hectares) at the confluence of four rivers that included the Trent. Vermuyden recruited c.200 families of Flemings, and French-speaking Walloons from what was then the Spanish Netherlands, who would both finance and undertake the work. From the start the local commoners bitterly resented the presence of these industrious and alien Strangers who established their own settlement at Sandtoft. Vermuyden was operating under Royal patronage, and so he and his fellow immigrants were under greater suspicion when the Civil War broke out. This resentment turned to violence; houses and drainage works were burnt down and the wooden windpumps and giant drainage screws, brought over from Holland, destroyed.

As at Dagenham, Vermuyden and his backers had been promised as their payment one third of the land to be reclaimed, but all they garnered from the Axholme disaster were bitter legal and financial disputes. Many of the Strangers therefore moved from Sandtoft and either returned to their home countries or moved south of the Wash to resettle around Thorney where Francis, the 4th Earl of Bedford, owned a large tract of fen which he wanted reclaimed.

Vermuyden, who had already worked for the Earl, was employed to drain the flooded fens and in 1630 began work with finance provided by his patron and thirteen other 'Gentlemen Adventurers', several of whom were Huguenot refugees from France. Vermuyden's grand design hinged on the cutting of a straight 70ft (21 metres) wide canal from Earith to Salters Lode, a distance of 21 miles (33 km). Ancillary to this major work were numerous straight cuts, dykes, and a catchwater channel that skirted the eastern rim of the fens. A controversial feature of the design was to divide the fens into three artificial 'levels'. A more effective device he introduced was to set aside low-lying 'washes' beside the main drainage channels which could absorb floods caused by exceptional rainfall, or tidal surges in the Wash. These flooded 'safety valves' provide sanctuary and feeding grounds for numberless waterfowl, especially migrant swans and geese in the winter months. The washes at Welney now afford enjoyment for birdwatchers who can view from the comfort of hides the annual pageant of the feeding of a great floodlit concourse of Whooper and Bewick's swans all of which, in Vermuyden's day, would have been fair game for the 'fen slodgers' who peopled the fens.

Vermuyden's plans may well have suited the drainage of his native marshes in Zeeland but they turned out to be less effective for the fens. Much of the reclaimed land continued to flood in winter and Skertchly, who was renowned as a local historian of the fens, declared that 'Vermuyden began badly, progressed ignorantly, and finished disastrously'. Harsh words indeed, recently proved unfair, as modern hydraulic engineers now regard the Dutchman's master plan as basically sound. Although Vermuyden received a knighthood from a grateful King, his financial backers were ruined and the Earl only survived because of his landed wealth. Thus was proved the truth of an old Dutch proverb – "The first farmer kills himself with work, the second lives in poverty, and only the third wins a livelihood".

The first engraved map of the Great Level of the fens was produced in 1632 by another Dutchman, Hondius from Amsterdam, and shows how one of the reclaimed areas in the Bedford Level was called 'Adventurers Fen', a sad reminder of a flawed but ambitious project.

The Civil War intervened and in 1649 William, the 5th Earl of Bedford, revived the reclamation schemes following a remarkable survey of c.310,000 acres (129,000 hectares) of virgin fen by a surveyor called Hayward. Work restarted and the New Bedford River was cut, parallel to the Old River, and the Denver sluices were constructed at the seaward end where both Rivers join. Vermuyden's parallel canals are now one of the few feats of human engineering that can be seen from outer space!

By 1652 the whole area bounded by Brandon, Wisbech and Peterborough was declared fit for cultivation. Today it is hard to appreciate how all the drainage channels were dug by gangs of navvies who called their work 'Jack Balling'. The men stood at various heights up the sloping sides of the cuts; those at the bottom dug out spadefuls of earth which were then passed to the men above who then, in turn, heaved them to those above them and so on until the spoil reached the top. Sometimes wooden barrows were filled at the bottom and then drawn up over narrow planks to the surface by ponies.

Villages near Huntingdon and Ely such as Fen Stanton and Fen Drayton became centres for the drainage works which employed c.10,000 men at the busiest times. There was always a shortage of labour and Dutch prisoners taken during the Anglo-Dutch naval battles were put to work. Many of the older buildings in these villages still display Flemish gabling and distinctive roof lines. Legend has it that Vermuyden stayed at Fen Drayton in a house that has carved over its front door the motto *'NIET ZONDER ARBEIT'* - translated as 'Nothing achieved without labour'.

The Anchor Inn at Sutton Gault in Cambridgeshire was once a hostel for Dutch workers, and local street names in other villages survive to commemorate the presence of the Strangers, such as 'Munnerstraat' in Ramsey. However, as at Axholme and Hatfield, the local inhabitants, who saw their traditional livelihood ebbing away as fast as the vanishing floodwaters, vented their frustration by sabotaging sluices and windpumps. The foundations of the restored postmill at Denver include brick from Vermuyden's shattered sluice gates.

The windpumps were introduced from the Netherlands where they had been in use since the fourteenth century, and on the fens a simpler 'smock' mill – so called because it resembled a woman wearing the traditional ankle-length wide skirts – was in common use. The first recorded use of a smock mill was at Holbeach in 1588; the paddles, powered by the sails, lifted the water from the smaller dykes into the main drainage channels. Where thousands of these windpumps once worked, today only one mill survives, at Herringfleet on the River Waveney on the Somerleyton estate. It was built in 1830 and worked right up to 1956. The four-sided 'smock' mill preserved at Wicken Fen, near Soham, was originally used by the diggers of the peat hags at Lapwing, part of Adventurers Fen. In 1955 the mill was moved to its present site where it was adapted to pump water into the fen so as to maintain the original wet land. Today extra help for maintaining the habitat is given by six, wild Dutch ponies, called *'konigs'* or *'tarpan'*, which roam the fen.

The steam engine invented by Watt replaced the windpumps both here and in the Netherlands and steam pumps were used by the Dutch to drain the Haarlemermeer, 19,000 hectares of flooded marsh, that became the site for Schiphol international airport. In time steam gave way to diesel and today all the pumps are driven by electricity.

The last stretch of water to be drained in the fens was Whittlesey Mere, near Thorney, which covered c.1,870 acres (750 hectares) in summer but in winter the surface area was nearly doubled. This was in 1850, 200 years after the Stuart monarchs, supported by their adventurous subjects, first pursued their expensive and ultimately successful ambitions to create fertile, dry pastures where none had ever existed before.

Chapter IV

THE HUMBLE HERRING
AND THE NORTH SEA

Over the centuries the sea has done more both to unite and divide the communities of East Anglia and the Low Countries than any other cause. Although not an island race, the Dutch have a long and intimate acquaintance with the sea of which they have become masters, especially the 'German Ocean', which we now call the North Sea, a name that derives from the Dutch '*Noord Zee*'. In the library of Blickling Hall in Norfolk there is a map of the North Sea, the work of the Dutch cartographer Donker in 1667, that records in careful detail the bearings and soundings that every mariner needed to ensure a safe passage across it.

The growth of sea-borne trade and the geographical discoveries of the sixteenth and seventeenth centuries generated a demand for such charts and maps which the Dutch were able to make with ever-increasing accuracy and precision. Mercator, whose real name was Gerhard Kremer, came from Flanders as did his close colleague, Ortelius. Together they freed geography from medieval superstition by employing mathematical principles. They produced the first map of the world with a unique projection that became the forerunner of scientific maps.

These maps and charts were engraved in Holland, as were Camden's 1564 map of the British Isles, and the county maps of England. Mercator was followed by two makers of hydrographic charts, Wagenaer and Blaeu, the accuracy of which made navigation around the shores of Europe infinitely safer. Wagenaer was himself a pilot of merchant ships trading from his home port of Enkhuizen on the Zuiderzee; he produced his first chart in 1584 which covered the coast from Holland to Cadiz. By 1598 his charts extended their coverage to Scotland and even as far north as the Arctic. They were

45

engraved on copper plate and printed at Leiden by Plantin who gave his name to an elegant and popular font that is used in this book.

In 1588 Wagenaer's works were translated into English under the title *'The Mariners Mirrour'* and became so indispensable to sailors that they were known as 'waggoners'. He was invited to join a committee appointed by the States General in Holland entrusted with the task of discovering a means of accurately measuring longitude while at sea. If only the Dutch scientist Christiaan Huygens had been able at that time to perfect a reliable method of compensating his marine clock, the longitude problem would have been solved a full century before Harrison's chronometer proved so successful.

The art of navigation as developed by the Dutch and Flemish had, within a century of the earliest voyages of exploration, determined the course of overseas development by rival colonial powers. From South Africa to the eastern seaboard of North America; from Australia and New Zealand to the East Indies, the Dutch established their trading posts. It was only because trade was not subordinated to colonial expansion that the Dutch bases were lost during disputes with the more belligerent powers.

Back in the 'German Ocean', the rivalry between the Dutch and the English centred on the industry that made fortunes for both countries – the pursuit of the humble herring, a fish named from the Old Norse *'haring'*. It was the sudden migration of herring in great shoals from the Baltic over 900 years ago that gave the fishermen of the Low Countries a chance to prove their supremacy. Herring, whether fresh, smoked or cured, rapidly became part of the staple diet, even for people who lived far from the coast. At Felsted, far inland in Essex, in the covered porch of a building beside the church, still remain the wooden hatches from which the herrings were sold in medieval times.

A 'Free Fair' for herring and other fish was held on the *'denes'* or dunes – from the Dutch *'duin'* – at the mouth of the River Yare in Norfolk between the eleventh and fourteenth centuries, and this helped to establish the port of 'Great Yare' or Yarmouth. Open-air fish fairs and markets continued to be popular well into the nineteenth century and these beach scenes became favourite subjects for the artists of the Norwich School of painters. George Vincent's 1821 painting '*the Dutch Fair on Yarmouth Beach*' is on display in the local museum as are many similar studies in the Castle Museum at Norwich, by John Crome, John Sell Cotman and other local artists.

The importance of the herring trade to Yarmouth was pithily expressed in the old jingle :

'Saint Patrike for Ireland
Saint George for England
The herring for Yarmouth'.

Lay subsidies provided by the government between 1524 and 1568 encouraged foreign merchants, especially the Dutch, to settle in east coast ports. Lowestoft, for ever the bitter rival of Yarmouth, attracted many who traded with other Hanse ports and a contemporary drawing of the waterfront in c.1785 shows several buildings with the distinctive 'shaped' gabling. Likewise, at Aldeburgh, overlooking the shingle beach, there remain several colourful buildings with their prominent gables.

Southwold has less pretentious 'Flemish' town houses but the old town pump in the market place is emblazoned with painted herrings, a reminder of the obligation recorded in Domesday, that the Lord of the Manor could claim an annual tribute of 25,000 herring from the port. Southwold once boasted a wicker-work, underwater weir which was used for trapping sprats and herring when it was too rough for the fishing boats to be launched.

The main herring season is a short one – from mid-September to mid-November. This is when the fish are in prime condition, full of either milt or roe; their fat content is also lower, all of which makes them more valuable than fish caught in the summer months. To catch them the fishermen used drift nets, known as 'flews', made from hempen or linen twine, with a mesh of c.1 inch (2.6 cm). About a hundred of these nets were joined together and hung at different depths, suspended from a master rope or 'warp' which was kept afloat by small wooden barrels or buoys. Each boat might 'shoot' 1800 metre of nets at one time.

The Dutch perfected the art of catching the herring and, just as important, of curing them while at sea so that the catch when landed would sell at a premium. The fishermen put to sea from their home ports such as Delft, Rotterdam and Schiedam in a fleet of blunt-bowed, sturdy boats of between 80 and 100 tons burden called *'busses'*. Each boat would have a crew of 10 to 20 men and boys, and, inland from Southwold today, the creek, which is the home of the local sailing club, is still called Buss Creek.

In the late fifteenth century a Fleming named Wilhelm Beukels devised an effective way of curing the herring; his method was to remove the guts and gills through a neat slit in the throat, and then pack the fish in layers or 'tiers' in barrels with salt sprinkled between each layer. Herrings thus packed were called 'white', or pickled, because of the pure quality white salt used in the process; they commanded a higher price than the fish prepared in the English ports. Each barrel contained 1000 fish and ten such barrels were called a 'last'. The Scottish women who migrated south each autumn to process the herring landed from the fishing fleets were famous for their dexterity, and for knowing exactly how many fish were in each barrel at any one time without actually having to count them!

The proverbial 'red' herring, an ungutted and pregnant fish, was a speciality produced at both Yarmouth and Lowestoft. The herring were first heaped on the floor of a smokehouse of Dutch design and then sprinkled with salt. They were left thus for two days before being washed, after which women called 'rivers' then threaded four-foot long 'speets' or spits through the mouth and gill cover of each fish. The loaded spits were then hung from wooden racks while fires of ash or oak billets were then kindled on the smokehouse floor. The fires were allowed to burn intermittently for a month. When smoked the fish were then packed, again 1,000 to a barrel, ready for exporting to far-flung ports such as Leghorn and Malaga in the Mediterranean. Red herring was much in demand for feeding soldiers on campaigns as well as slaves toiling on the plantations in the West Indies.

Men and women, now in their eighties, remember when, as children, their fathers took red herrings to work as part of their midday meal. Many houses kept a small barrel of these herrings in the larder throughout the winter; after the salt was washed off the fish were grilled or toasted on open fires.

There remain one or two traditional smokehouses in Lowestoft which produce the red herring and it was a proud native of that town, one Thomas Nash, who wrote at the end of the sixteenth century a piece called:

'The Lenten Stuffe – or the praise of the Red Herring'.

The herring industry depended upon regular supplies of timber and therefore woodland, in the hinterland, was coppiced in the traditional ten to fourteen year cycle in order to supply staves for the barrels and billets for the smokehouses. There remain several medieval woods in East Anglia where the art of coppicing is being revived to meet the demand from water authorities for bundles of faggots used for protecting the banks of rivers and dykes.

Salt was also needed in great quantities and much of it came from salt pans sited on many of the coastal marshes. This explains why the word 'salt' appears in many place-names around the east coast – grey salt in particular was produced in pans along the River Tyne and its estuary. Top quality white salt was imported from pans along the shore of the Bay of Biscay.

The herring fishermen also caught mackerel in the summer, and then sailed further north in search of cod whose livers, saved during the gutting process on board the boats, were a valuable commodity. The livers were boiled down in great copper cauldrons sited on the open dunes – Lowestoft was well known for the strong smell that wafted up into the town. The cod liver oil, known as train oil after the Dutch word *'traen'*, was much in demand for lamps and tanning leather, as well as for curing stomach upsets in humans.

Sadly, the herring is now in serious decline due to many

years of uncontrolled over-fishing but belated measures enforced by the European Union should enable the herring to survive, a fish that has done so much to strengthen the bonds between fishing communities around the North Sea.

The Dutch are very partial to smoked eel and for centuries there has been a brisk trade from King's Lynn of eels trapped in the fens and shipped to Holland. Similarly there were exports of shrimps, netted in the Wash, and exported from Wisbech, Lynn, and smaller ports.

Although as early as the 1570s a regular ferry service was running from Nieuwport in Holland to Norwich via Great Yarmouth, it was Harwich, in Essex, that became the main gateway to the Low Countries, and the terminus for the first official mail service between this country and Europe. In 1661 twice-weekly sailings were started so that diplomatic 'packets' could be sent with some security between Harwich and Hellevoetsluis in Holland. This service, which was finally suspended in 1831, became an indispensable conduit for trading and market intelligence between the *beurs* (Bourse) in Amsterdam and merchants in London. All passengers wishing to board the packet had to have a 'pass-port' which is how this travel document first came to be used. And the word 'packet' is now widely used to describe vessels that provide regular mail and ferry services throughout the world.

Maritime terms such as '*anker*' (anchor) and '*jacht*' (yacht) are freely shared between British and Dutch sailors as many originated in the Old Norse language spoken by the marauding Vikings. One particular expression dates back to the period when the hated Duke of Alva, the henchman of Philip II of Spain, was sent to subdue the Netherlands. The Duke was tall, thin, and tough – just like the *dukdalf*, the term used by Dutch bargees for a wooden mooring post.

Chapter V

FARMING AND HUSBANDRY

In the year 1500 there were under three million people living in England and Wales; by 1700 the population had risen to five and a half million, all but a million of whom relied upon the countryside for a living. This great increase and the start of the drift to the towns meant that farmers had to produce more food and accelerated the speed at which the medieval open fields and wastes were enclosed. Enclosures enabled both the sheep farmers and the cereal growers to enjoy their full potential for the first time.

Before the Dissolution of the religious houses the monks were the most scientific farmers of the day and close contact with their brethren in Europe enabled them to benefit from improved methods of cultivation. A century later, European farming again encouraged British farmers to experiment, and a book entitled '*Four Bookes of Husbandrie*' by Barnaby Googe, published in 1577, made farmers take note of what was happening elsewhere. The book was in fact a translation of a work by a writer from the Netherlands called Heresbach.

Another translator of Dutch treatises on agriculture was Antony Ashley, the grandfather of the Earl of Shaftesbury, who had to escape to Holland following his implication in the Rye House Plot against William III. Ashley lived for a time in the Netherlands as a contemporary of the famous cartographer Waganaer (see Chapter III) some of whose important works he also translated. His other claim to fame was to introduce the cabbage plant into England.

The Civil War forced into exile a number of English landowners with Royalist sympathies and one of these was Sir Richard Weston who sought refuge in Flanders. There he noticed how the local farmers on the poorer land between Ghent and Antwerp were able to raise excellent crops by using a simple rotation of flax, turnips and oats, which were undersown with clover. On his return home in 1645 Sir Richard recorded his observations under the title '*A Discourse of Husbandrie used in Brabant and Flanders*'. A copy of his manuscript was published by the unscrupulous Samuel Hartlib in 1650, and in it was described for the first time how the turnips and clover were fed to livestock in the winter thus making it unnecessary to slaughter the animals at the onset of winter as was the universal custom. Weston also commended the Flemish custom of tenants 'taking a Farm upon Improvement' which meant that on the expiry of the usual twenty-one year lease a tenant would be compensated for any improvements he may have made to the farm during his tenancy.

The Flemish also cultivated sainfoin, a forage crop often undersown with cereals. The name derives from the medieval French and Latin words '*sanum faenum*' meaning 'wholesome hay'. A tract extolling the benefits and cultivation of this valuable crop was published in 1669 but it was Heresbach who was the first writer to mention 'Burgundian grass' as well as rape, turnips and a simple reaping machine. He also stressed the great importance of manure, echoing the truth of the old Norfolk proverb 'Muck is the mother of money'.

Turnips had been grown in the Low Countries and Germany long before Weston wrote about their first arrival in East Anglia when they were descibed as 'turnepez'. The Dutch and Flemish Strangers were the first to grow these root vegetables in their allotments outside Norwich and other towns such as Colchester. The first large landowner in this country to exploit this new crop was Viscount Townshend, a Whig politician who was for a time the British ambassador to the United Provinces. In 1695 he inherited a large estate in north Norfolk which enabled him to experiment with European farming methods.

The tradition of husbandry 'Turnip' Townshend inherited was based on the 'open field' system under which the landlords' sheep grazed the open heaths in the summer and the stubble on the cultivated strips during the winter. This winter 'shackage' ceased to be available as soon as turnips were grown as keep for the livestock. Sown in the autumn the roots, when ready for lifting in the early summer, were often left in the ground so that sheep could be folded on them. The owner of the field would then benefit from the sheep's manure, the traditional 'golden hoof'. Either way, the livestock had to be kept off the fields while the roots grew which meant enclosing the cultivated land with thorn hedges and wooden paling, a practice that gave rise to the prophecy of 1604 – 'Horne and Thorne shall make England forlorne'.

Between 1720 and 1840, as four and a half million acres of land were enclosed by over 200,000 miles of hedges, the rural landscape was irrevocably transformed in the best interests of landowners wanting to increase their output by crop rotation and new breeds of livestock. The introduction of the Norfolk four-course 'shift' was made that much easier through the invention by Jethro Tull of his revolutionary turnip drill. He was the son of a Berkshire landowner and renowned for being a scholar, a lawyer, a traveller and a musician. He finally settled down to become an innovative farmer and used his knowledge of the mechanics of the organ, which he played well, to make a drill that could sow three different seeds without mixing them, and at varying depths. Thus clover and sainfoin could be undersown with barley or wheat, or vice-versa.

But first the fields had to be ploughed and the introduction of the light 'Dutch' plough made the work of cultivation much easier. The first reference to such a plough occurs in Googe's '*First Book of Husbandrie*' in which he describes how in Holland the ground is 'excellently well plowed' with two horses 'going very softly' and comments that 'the like is used in Norfolk and Lincoln'. Blith, in 1653, talks about the 'Dutch or Norfolk' plough, drawn by two horses, which had first appeared in the eastern counties. Up to the time of the Reformation the cumbersome eight-oxen plough was used both in the Low Countries and Britain which explains why so many open field boundaries were shaped like a backward 'S'. The length

from the nose of the leading ox
to the point of the plough share
could be as much as forty five
feet and to plough out a
headland with no curve would
have meant encroaching on the
neighbour's land.

An early 19th century swing plough.
(Norfolk Rural Life Museum, Gressenhall)

The introduction of the light, horse-drawn swing or wheelless plough allowed of straight field boundaries which began first to appear in the Low Countries after the Reformation, and then later across the North Sea. By 1721 the Norfolk plough had wheels and a cast iron share while in Suffolk the preference was for an improved, curved mould board. With either plough a ploughman using a two-horse team was able to cultivate an acre a day. Improvements to these basic ploughs were made by adopting further Dutch expertise, examples being the Rotherham plough, patented in 1730, and a similar implement designed by a Norfolk farmer, Arbuthnot.

The campaign to adopt 'turnip husbandry' was also given a boost by Arthur Young, the first secretary to the Board of Agriculture established by William Pitt in 1793. Young compiled a 'Domesday Book' of the land following years of travelling throughout the country on his blind, grey horse and the resultant *'Annals of Agriculture'* paints a vivid picture of the contemporary farming scene. George III – 'Farmer George' – said of Young 'I am more obliged to you than to any man in my Dominions'. At last the humble turnip had received the accolade of royalty!

In 1776 Thomas William Coke inherited the Holkham estate of 45,000 acres (18,300 hectares) on the north Norfolk coast and declared that 'the King of Denmark is my nearest neighbour'. He was determined to improve the farming methods of his tenants and thereby increase his rental income. As a measure of his ensuing success the annual rental rose from £2,200 in 1776 to £20,000 in 1816. He did not just stop at introducing crop rotation; his programme of livestock improvement was equally far-reaching and effective. He replaced the herds of Shorthorn cattle with a North Devon breed and created the Suffolk sheep by breeding from the Norfolk Horn, Southdown and Border Leicester strains. At the same time he took several of his farms 'in hand' and reclaimed large areas of coastal marshland.

Coke's celebrated annual 'sheep shearings' which he started in 1778 were used to publicise his revolutionary farming methods, first amongst his tenants and then among farmers from all over the country. The Emperor of Russia even sent his special emissary to the 1816 gathering at Holkham which was attended by over 600 guests for a whole week. Even so, Coke reckoned that his new ideas only spread at the rate of half a mile a year so suspicious were farmers of the new-fangled ideas. He even sent into Gloucestershire a Norfolk plough together with a ploughman and a pair of horses to prove that this team could do as much work in a day as a traditional team of two men, a boy and six horses.

A century later another root crop, this time introduced by the Dutch, was to transform once again the arable farming scene in East Anglia. The first crystals of sugar from beet were extracted in Silesia in c.1747 and farmers in France, Germany and the Low Countries began to cultivate 'sugar' beet as a valuable cash crop. Unlike Britain, Europe did not have access to cheap supplies of cane sugar, so home-grown beet became even more valuable and heavily subsidised because of the disruption of foreign trade during the Anglo-French wars.

The Dutch were the first to seize the opportunity to grow and process beet in East Anglia where soil conditions promised to be very suitable. In 1884 a factory to process beet was built at Lavenham in Suffolk but it soon failed. In 1911 a group of Dutch capitalists established a new factory at Cantley, near Acle in Norfolk, with machinery imported from Dordrecht in Holland. Slicing of beet began the following year and, in order to guarantee a sufficient supply of beet for the plant, the Dutch bought farms in the vicinity. This factory was sold in 1916 to the Anglo-Netherlands Sugar Company which resumed work in an enlarged plant at Cantley in 1920.

The British Government helped to create a domestic beet sugar industry by offering farmers direct subsidies and Empire preference, a policy that has benefited growers ever since. The beet factory at Wissington, on the banks of the River Wissey near Downham Market in Norfolk, was built in 1925 on the site of a failed enterprise which had the object of extracting ammonia from the peat and vegetation removed during drainage works in the surrounding fens. By 1936 there were fifteen beet processing plants which in that year merged to become the British Sugar Company. Today, Norfolk accounts for one third of the national acreage down to beet; Suffolk and Cambridgeshire have each a tenth share of the total. Both as a cash and catch crop beet is now indispensable to East Anglian farmers, an industry employing c.23,000 people at all stages of production and needing over 700,000 lorry loads to convey the annual crop from farm to factory.

The drainage of the great fens around the Wash in the latter half of the seventeenth century by the Earl of Bedford and his fellow merchant venturers, many of whom were exiled French Huguenots, attracted many Flemish and Walloon farmers to the reclaimed, fertile acres. These immigrants settled around Thorney, near Peterborough, where the ruined abbey was partially repaired to provide a place of worship for the Protestant Strangers. They had brought with them the seeds of a bitter, cabbage-like plant with bright green leaves called '*koollzaad*' by the Dutch and colza or coleseed by the English. This was an early form of the rapeseed plant that now, in early summer, turns much of the countryside into a chequerboard of brilliant yellow and green.

Colza was traditionally sown in August and harvested in June the following year. The oil extracted from the pods was used both as lamp oil and for softening spun wool before it was woven. The fenland was ideal for this crop the cultivation of which required the use of a 'French' or paring plough. This enabled the farmer to skim off the top two to three inches of soil and grass which was then gathered into small heaps and burnt. To try and prevent the underlying peaty soil igniting, the ashes were spread over the ground and ploughed in at the first opportunity. But as this practice inevitably caused many peat fires the Constable of Thorney eventually banned it and many of the farmers moved elsewhere.

At the beginning of the sixteenth century another plant introduced from the Netherlands was to change for ever the drinking habits of the British. Hops, a form of hemp, was used in Europe to make 'beer', a drink with a more bitter taste than the traditional ale drunk in vast quantities in this country. Hops also gave a better preservative quality to beer. The oft repeated jingle -

'Hops, Reformation and Beer
Came into England all in one year'-

was certainly true in one sense but hops certainly preceded the Reformation. By 1573, when Tusser promulgated his *'Five Hundred Pointes of Good Husbandrie'*, he reported that hops were widely grown in Suffolk, and in 1552 Edward VI legislated for the proper control of their culture. The district around Beccles was especially suited for growing hemp and hops.

The Low Countries have for long had a great influence on the farming livestock of this country. The black Flemish horse was the ancestor of most of Britain's heavy draught breeds, and the Fries Melksschaap was a breed of milksheep that exceeded any other in milk production. As far back as the fourteenth century the dairy industry relied on sheep rather than cattle and the Old English term for a sheep dairy was 'wick'. Places such as Monkswick and Northwick were those where the milking flocks were once centred. The sheep's milk was turned into a durable cheese which was exported to Holland and Zeeland. Although re-introduced to Britain in the 1960s, the Melksschaap has long been the preferred dairy breed throughout the Mediterranean, in South Africa and South America.

The popular black-and-white breed of dairy cattle, first introduced as the Holstein and then known as the Friesian, has been steadily improved by careful selection, helped by the importation of stock bulls from the Netherlands and South Africa. Just as the Longhorn cattle in Britain were superseded by the

Shorthorns, so the most successful dairy breed in the twentieth century has been the Friesian-Holstein. We wonder what will be the dominant breeds in the next century?

There appeared in the 1930s on most English farms a simple, open-sided barn with a curved, corrugated iron roof set on tall steel or wooden uprights. This was the Dutch barn and in East Anglia a curious rumour accompanied the barn's introduction. It was whispered that the barns could be used as aircraft hangars in wartime and so were sited beside potential enemy landing strips. Maybe this was just a story good for a pint of beer at the local pub!

The traditional way of topping beet on a farm at West Barsham, Norfolk, in c.1918.
(Norfolk Rural Life Museum, Gressenhall)

Picking turnips in a frosty field in 1985 - Snetterton, Norfolk.
(Norfolk Rural Life Museum, Gressenhall)

Two Friesian heifers that were shown at an Agricultural Show sometime in the mid-20's.
(Norfolk Rural Life Museum, Gressenhall)

An old-fashioned way of checking the daffodil bulbs at Spalding, c.1948.
(Norfolk Rural Life Museum, Gressenhall)

The parterre in the Dutch style at Wimpole Hall, Cambridgeshire.

The dahlia garden at Anglesey Abbey, near Cambridge, which is planted up with Dutch hyacinths in the spring.

Bust of CLUSIUS, founder and designer of the
botanical garden at Leiden, and of which he
was the Prefect from 1593 until his death
in 1609.

HUMPHRY REPTON - the first landscape
gardener; a drawing by an unknown artist.

A marquetry William and Mary table with a floral design which
includes birds, POWIS CASTLE.
(© National Trust Photographic Library/John Hammond)

A field of daffodils in Norfolk.

A colourful display of tulips at Springfields Gardens, Spalding.

The Orangery at Ickworth House, Suffolk.

Chapter VI

TREES AND FLOWERS

The emigrants from the Netherlands, the Strangers, brought with them not only their skills and their faith; they also came with their love of flowers and gardens. They organised the first ever 'florist feasts', held in Norwich in 1631, with the object of showing off to others all the different flowers and vegetables that were grown on their allotments.

The Dutch in the sixteenth and seventeenth centuries were pre-eminent in the procurement of plants, many of which came from the far-flung territories where the Dutch had trading stations. One such collector was Hieronymus van Beverninck, who discovered the nasturtium in Peru in 1684.

The Dutch were also the pioneers of plant propagation and established a botanical study garden as early as 1590 at Leiden University. Carolus Clusius, a great botanist, was the first Prefect of the garden and was responsible for laying down the fundamental principles of descriptive botany. He also introduced the tulip to Europe, via Turkey, having found the flower growing wild in Persia. The first tulip bulbs were sent to Austria in the diplomatic bag and thence to Holland: the descendants of those bulbs still thrive in the botanic garden at Leiden.

The speed with which 'tulipomania' gripped the Netherlands and France, although well documented, is even now hard to appreciate. By 1636 the value of a single bulb that could produce a striped 'Rembrandt' tulip flower reached such bizarre heights that investors - they were really gamblers – would gladly exchange even their dwellings for one. In the following year the market as suddenly collapsed and fortunes were lost. Ironically it was the diseased bulb that created the prized bloom and today we can enjoy those rich-coloured stripes through the medium of the still-life paintings of such masters as Jan van Huysum who died in 1749.

The tulip has long enjoyed a special place in the annals of gardening. Societies dedicated to tulip cultivation were first established in 1710 and to this day at least one such society remains active. Charles I instructed that over fifty varieties of tulip were to be planted in the royal gardens and two centuries later, when formal garden layouts were all the fashion, serried ranks of Dutch tulips and daffodils supplied just the displays needed.

To meet this increased demand bulb growing began around Spalding in Lincolnshire in c.1890. The Dutch growers had long coveted the fertile, alluvial soils around the Wash and they now began to come over, first to sell bulbs, and then to stay and grow them. Cornelius Shooter was one of the first to settle and his descendants still live near Spalding. Dominicus van Konynberg was another who came over from Noordwyk in 1922, followed by the Geest brothers, John and Leonard, who started their very successful careers by pedalling around on their bicycles selling bulbs. An Englishman, Dick Wellband, was also a cyclist – he won races on his penny-farthing – and was one of the first growers to study commercial bulb production in Holland.

It was soon realised that growing bulbs was a business ideally suited for small holdings run with family labour, and so expansion in the Spalding-Wisbech area was rapid. The Darwin tulip cultivars were first introduced in 1905 and by 1920 the first glasshouses for forcing bulbs were in use. In 1913 so many varieties were being grown that the Royal Horticultural Society appointed a committee, made up of British and Dutch experts, to determine a common nomenclature.

During the two world wars many of the bulb fields were turned over to vegetable production, with a nucleus of the prized bulbs being carefully preserved. And during the 1939-45 war daffodil and tulip bulbs were scrupulously cleaned before being sent to the U.S.A to help establish a bulb industry over there. Meanwhile, in Holland, any spare tulip bulbs were boiled in order to make a nutritious soup which was fed to cattle, pigs and starving humans. Not daffodil bulbs, however, as they are poisonous.

The Dutch remain the major suppliers of the smaller bulbs as harvesting mechanically in the sandy soils prevalent in the Netherlands is less damaging and therefore more productive. Water-table management, for bulbs as for potatoes, is also crucial; it is a skill which the Dutch growers have perfected over the centuries.

The English fen growers however suffer from one disadvantage that does not trouble the Dutch – the wily and fast-flying fen pheasants like nothing better than a juicy tulip bulb; and the more rare the cultivar the better it seems to taste.

Holland is justly proud of the famous Keukenhof bulb gardens, an international showpiece for the industry, but Spalding can be as proud of its own gardens at Springfields, albeit on a smaller scale. Likewise the renowned Spalding flower parade, first organised in 1958 with expert Dutch help, copies the colourful Corso in Holland. Now every year on the first Saturday in May the many floats, covered in a myriad spring blooms of every colour, process along a four and a half mile route around the town.

Four centuries after Clusius the importance of floriculture remains a vital part of the Dutch economy. In the year 2000 the Dutch share of the world trade was 59% in cut flowers and 48% for plants, an overall value of six billion US dollars. Over 57,000 people are employed full-time in floriculture and another 15,000 keep the industry supplied with all the materials required. Even today it is usual for British nurseries to send seed over to the Netherlands for their nurseries to propagate; the seedlings are then exported for sale in the garden centres.

We have seen how the Dutch and Flemish have clawed back from the sea so much valuable land, every square metre of which has to be used intensively. This explains the 'Dutchness' of garden design which is identified by the use of small compartments and neatness, features which are well exemplified in East Anglian gardens. Gardens become open 'boxes' surrounded by thick hedges to keep out the 'lazy' north-east winds that sweep in from the Arctic. The

Dutch liked to make more of a plain hedge by weaving cut flowers into the foliage, or even hanging on them small panels of coloured glass. These sheltered or 'secret' gardens usually had a sundial as their focal point and a gazebo in one corner for relaxation. A perfect example of such a garden, surrounded by tall beech hedges, is at Blickling Hall in Norfolk.

At East Ruston, within a mile of the windswept north-east coast of Norfolk, a superb garden has been created with the varying compartments all filled with a surprising array of tender plants.

Water in some form is usually present in a true 'Dutch' garden. There are a few East Anglian gardens where remain the short 'canals' or rectangular ponds, fringed by evergreens such as cypress and yew in formal array, and overlooked from either end by brick pavilions or summer houses. In the garden of the Old Hall at Aylsham in Norfolk such a water feature still survives.

The Dutch have always shown a mystical respect for the orange, a citrus that would certainly perish without artificial warmth and shelter during the harsh Low Country winters. So the Dutch first invented the stove house at the beginning of the seventeenth century, a building that developed into the later ornate orangeries. Within these structures of brick, glass and timber both tender and citrus plants could be kept safe over the winter, planted in their own individual wooden tubs for ease of transporting. The pitch of the orangery roof was an optimum fifty two degrees and heat was generated by flued stoves, invented by the Dutch and further developed by the Germans.

The idea of the glazed orangery *(see page 109)* soon caught on in Britain and scarce an imposing mansion or manor was built without one. It is a sad reflection on the present decline of the country house that so few orangeries remain in good repair and used for their original purposes; many are now tea rooms or merely extra storage space.

The Flemish Strangers from the Spanish Netherlands were also some of the first and most skilled exponents of the forced and intensive cultivation of fruit and vegetables, using glass cloches, lean-to greenhouses and raised beds. Doubtless the seeds of the first Brussels sprouts came with them as well! And it is no coincidence that the greatest concentration of serpentine or 'crinkle-crankle' walls is found in Norfolk and Suffolk; walls cleverly designed to make the most of our fickle climate to ripen the fruit grown against them.

The Dutch started with the priceless advantage of soils that had been enriched by the silt dredged from the deepened dykes, and by peat from further inland. The resultant fine tilth was ideal for intensive cultivation for plants and trees.

On land which is almost flat the trees and their important shadows are needed to give character and perspective to the landscape. The planting and strategic siting of trees has therefore always been of enormous importance to the Dutch who, for centuries, have led the way in silviculture. Old prints show how live, mature trees were transplanted successfully by first pruning the roots and then binding them with protective balls of earth in special baskets. The whole trees were then transported on open carts drawn by a span of oxen.

The common lime, *tilia x vulgaris 'pallida'*, was a favourite tree in the Netherlands not only because of its fragrant flowers and red-fringed shoots but also for the prolific basal shoots which were used for easy propagation. The British imported these young lime whips for planting up the great avenues around their country houses in the early 1700s. A fine example of such a lime avenue can still be admired at Rougham in north Norfolk; although planted as early as 1691 it still has only a few gaps. The uniformity of growth achieved with these limes was a useful selling point for the Dutch nurserymen. The Dutch elm, *ulmus x Hollandica,* was also much in demand for avenues which were finally destroyed by the elm disease that swept through the country at the end of the twentieth century.

For hedges, and the ornamental *broderie* and *parterre* gardens, the Dutch box, *buxus sempervirens* L *suffruticosa* was very popular until at least c.1701 when locally grown box became available.

The Dutch even found uses for the wild reeds and rushes growing in the marshes and the dykes. Part of a cargo shipped from

Rotterdam in the sixteenth century was described as 'bullrushes' and reed was a regular export, used for thatching. Rushes are still imported from Holland to meet the demands of the Waveney Rush industry based in south Norfolk where woven rush matting and baskets are made to designs that hark back to Anglo-Saxon times.

It was Humphry Repton who first made the clear distinction between the straightforward growing of fruit, flowers and vegetables-horticulture; and the wider concept of a managed landscape. He coined the phrase 'landscape gardening' in 1788 when, aged 36, he began his successful career as the creator of many majestic landscapes. Born in Suffolk and educated in Norwich, he was sent to Holland by his father in 1764 to learn the language in readiness for a career in trade with the Netherlands. But he soon realised that trade was not for him and instead he took every opportunity to visit the Dutch gardens and parks, his sketchbook in hand. He noted how the gardens displayed 'small scale neatness in the pleasure ground' and that 'true taste in landscape gardening is not an accidental effect'. Even more importantly, he linked art to the landscape as creating it 'can only be perfected by the united powers of the landscape painter and the practical gardener', two professions at which the Netherlanders already excelled. There is no doubt that Repton's early exposure to the parterres, knot gardens and imaginative tree planting in Holland influenced his designs for the commissions that were soon to follow, and set him apart from his equally renowned predecessor, Lancelot 'Capability' Brown.

Chapter VII

'FREE TRADE'

By calling themselves 'free traders', the eighteenth century smugglers contrived to give their law-breaking activities some legitimacy, and this helped them to rely on the support of the local population without which they could hardly operate. Cheating the Excise officers, or 'boat men' as they were called, was so widespread as scarcely to be regarded as a crime, as the taxation of the small luxuries of life encouraged otherwise law-abiding folk to evade paying the crippling duties imposed by impecunious governments. And around 1830, when agricultural workers were experiencing severe hardship, indulging in 'free trade' was a good way of flouting authority and improving their lot.

The impost now known as 'duty' was first introduced by the Normans, and was the ancestor of the tax on wool exports levied during the Middle Ages. The earliest systematic accounts of the wool trade date only from the reign of Edward I (1272-1307) during which most wool was shipped from Boston and London to the Netherlands and Italy. By 1353 only Boston, Yarmouth and Norwich were designated staple ports through which wool and cloth had to be exported. As the long-stapled wool from British flocks was second only to Spanish wool for quality, and therefore much in demand by Flemish weavers, it was not surprising that smuggling flourished. Customs Houses were built at the staple ports and equipped with massive scales called the 'King's Beams' and even today the headquarters of the Customs and Excise service is called King's Beam House.

The traders who exported the wool, needed to fill the holds of their vessels with return cargoes, and they quickly developed a thriving business in smuggling contraband, especially into east coast ports. The creeks and lonely, muddy shores around the coast proved ideal for 'running' smuggled goods; in Essex alone the estuaries of 22 rivers provided over 140 places suitable for landing goods when the tides were right. Further north, along the shores of Norfolk and Suffolk, the low cliffs bordering the shingle beaches were well supplied with gaps through which the trains of pack horses, their panniers laden with contraband, could find their way inland.

Following the imposition of steep import duties by the Commonwealth in 1649, to help finance the Anglo-Dutch wars and other campaigns, smuggling became big business. Joint stock companies were floated: Dutch and English investors were invited to buy company shares at between ten and twenty pounds each. The money thus raised financed the purchase of goods for 'export' to England. The trade soon became so lucrative that well-organised gangs on both sides of the North Sea were able to afford the loss of whole shipments and still make a handsome profit overall. Then, as now, alcohol in some form was included in most cargoes. To meet the demand the Dutch set up distilleries at Schiedam to produce potent gin, known as 'jenever' or 'Holland', while the Flemish and French supplied brandy through Dunkirk and other channel ports.

The most valuable contraband, however, was tea. In the year 1652 tea, as well as coffee and cocoa, began to be imported in quantity by the East India Company. The ambitious and enterprising officers working for 'John Company', as it was usually called, had the right to some free tonnage on the Company's vessels with which to trade as they pleased. As space aboard was at a premium, the favourite commodity was tea which could command the highest price. Smugglers were given the first option to buy the tea, and were thus able to offer tea of a better quality than the legally imported variety which, at that time, attracted duty of over 100%.

As a measure of the instant popularity of tea, legal imports amounted to over fifty tons by 1700 at a wholesale price of £2 per pound, but, by 1800, 4,000 tons a year were being imported, the price having dropped to two shillings a pound.

In addition, import duties were levied on a whole range of dry goods which included even such necessities as tallow for candles. As all sections of the population were affected by these duties, there was every incentive for people to connive at the import of contraband, especially when there was invariably a small reward in kind for the farmers, the millers, and even the clerics who provided labour, transport, and hiding places for the kegs, barrels, and packages that came ashore at night. Much appreciated were French ribbons for the wife, and a small barrel of brandy for the husband.

Before the establishment of a centralised customs service, the collection of duties was farmed out to the local gentry, who were expected to exploit the system and thereby provide themselves with a steady income. Even the poet William Wordsworth in Westmorland was a grateful recipient of such a sinecure. The smugglers, therefore, could carry on their 'free trade' with little risk of capture; all they needed to do was to reward the local 'establishment' for turning a blind eye to their clandestine activities. Rudyard Kipling, in his *'Smugglers' Song'*, graphically described how it was best for all good folk to stay behind closed doors when the smugglers went about their unlawful business.

Parson Woodforde, the much-respected incumbent of the parish of Weston Longville, a few miles west of Norwich, lived in the parsonage there from 1776 to 1803. His Diary proves that he was not averse to relying upon 'the honest smuggler Andrew' to keep him supplied with 'Holland and the best coniac'.

'Holland' gin also featured in a letter from one Edward Fitzgerald, the Suffolk poet and scholar, in which he tells of kegs of contraband gin being hidden under the altar cloth of the church at Theberton in Suffolk after they had been landed at Sizewell Gap, a favoured haunt of smugglers. An official report of a landing in June, 1746, is a vivid indication of the scale of the prevalent smuggling operations. Over two tons of tea, as well as a quantity of brandy, made up a cargo the successful landing of which required the secret co-operation of over eighty people in the Theberton parish. In 1778 another gang landed 300 casks of 'Holland' for which six large carts were needed to transport the cargo inland. In 1833 Excise men and coastguards at Kelling, on the north Norfolk coast, thwarted a landing in which over a hundred smugglers with twenty carts were involved; a smuggler was shot and killed during the encounter, and next morning the beach was found littered with over 200 casks and packages of brandy and tobacco.

At King's Lynn, a thriving port with good connections to London and the Midlands, the King's Excise Officers were based at the Customs House, built in 1683 as a copy of a typical Dutch harbour weigh house. This historic building is now faithfully restored and stands beside the Purfleet, an inlet recently dredged and once again a safe berth for small vessels. Lynn was a natural centre for smuggling and the Revenue men carried out constant checks on all imported commodities. The smugglers, therefore, went to great lengths to conceal their contraband as witness a report of 1677 by the Collector at Wells-next-the-Sea, who discovered 'fine goods hidden under pantiles, bottles, fencing pales, and chairs'. Another favourite ruse was to fill waterproofed barrels with goods and then drop them in shallow waters off-shore. When the 'coast was clear', the barrels were then retrieved. The crews of the regular Harwich 'packet' boats were constantly doing this on their return from the Dutch ports; the fleets of small craft used for dredging the oyster beds nearby afforded ideal camouflage for a smuggler searching for his sunken barrels.

In Harwich can be seen some of the handsome town houses which were used by the smugglers; these houses had interconnecting cellars that allowed for the rapid dispersal of goods if an emergency arose. The cellars were also a convenient way of avoiding the detested Press gangs as they sought to capture unwary sailors.

Overlooking the Orwell estuary, a mile downstream from Ipswich and near the present Yacht Clubhouse, is the Cathouse, a Gothic-style cottage so named because of the white cat that was once placed by the window at night as a signal to the smugglers that it was safe for them to land their goods.

Flemish weavers, settled at Blythburgh on the Suffolk coast,

exported their cloth in vessels that tied up at the quay beside the White Hart Inn, a building with a dubious past and a distinctive, shaped Flemish gable. It is easy to imagine how, as the creek filled at high tide, the dank cellars of the inn would have been crammed with contraband goods.

During the eighteenth century, the 'free traders' were in the ascendant and could count on much local sympathy for their activities. The Excise men, later supported by small detachments of dragoons, had an uphill and often thankless task in their efforts to outwit the smugglers. It was a dangerous game as both sides were heavily armed and ready for a fight. As the penalties for smuggling became harsher – transportation for many years was not unusual – clashes between the contestants were increasingly desperate, and so smugglers resorted to intimidation of the local population in order to safeguard their clandestine activities. But as the duty on tea was drastically reduced and the Excise presence much strengthened, smuggling became far less profitable.

A Coast Guard service was founded in 1822, and then handed over to the Admiralty thirty four years later, having effectively run the 'free traders' out of business. By 1841 the Collector at King's Lynn was able to claim that smuggling had all but ceased.

Human greed does not change, however, and there are always those who are out to make a quick profit by smuggling in goods for which there is a ready market. At the start of the new millennium tobacco products and drugs are the lucrative contraband; smuggling continues along the lonelier stretches of the coast, only now the modern 'free traders' use the power boat and small aircraft in place of the silent yawls and sloops of the past.

Chapter VIII

VIII

DECOYS

Wildfowl thrive on swamps and marshes and, before land reclamation began in the Fens, their flocks were immense. Wild ducks were a much-prized delicacy and at a time when religious observation was a way of life, duck was also a very important alternative to meat. In particular the pintail, the teal and the garganey breeds were not regarded as meat and therefore could be eaten during Lent.

The marsh dwellers of the Netherlands were as skilled as the Fenmen in exploiting the duck and one way of catching them was to stretch long, enveloping nets over the water into which the birds were driven. Then the Dutch refined the art of ensnaring duck by using the decoy which became increasingly effective as the areas of open marsh inexorably diminished. The word 'decoy' derives from the Dutch *'eendekooy'*, meaning a trap or cage for a duck, a word that became corrupted as 'duck-coy'.

Ideally, at each corner of a sheltered, small lake, were built semi-circular tunnels made from arched canes covered with netting. These 'pipes' were slightly curved, and tapered to a narrow detachable bag net at one end. Screens made of rushes in timber frames were then erected in a staggered line beside the pipes and connected with low wattle hurdles.

To lure the wild duck, the decoyman put tame, pinioned ducks on the lake and these were trained to swim towards the mouths of the pipes. Much depended on the wind direction so there were usually at least four pipes which enabled the decoyman to choose the one that best suited the prevailing wind. Grain or old potatoes thrown into the shallow water attracted the ducks to the mouth of the selected pipe. The decoyman's dog or 'piper' then appeared from behind the nearest screen and, because its coat was tawny like that of a fox, the duck swam towards it, consumed with curiosity. The well-trained dog then hopped over the first hurdle nearest the lake - and immediately disappeared behind a screen. The Dutch even have a name for this first hurdle, 'yackoop' - probably a corruption of the Dutch 'opjakkeren' meaning to 'chase up'.

The raft of duck, ever more intrigued, would swim down the pipe, following the dog as it kept appearing from behind the screens and leaping over successive hurdles. When the duck were well down the pipe the decoyman suddenly appeared at its mouth whereupon the birds panicked and flew into the net at the narrow end. It was then easy to lift them out and wring their necks.

The Dutch developed a special breed of dog, with a reddish coat of course, to work in the decoys - it was called a 'kooikerhondje'. The breed survives and is now registered. History relates how decoymen, without a proper 'piper' dog, used as a substitute whatever animal that came to hand and these included both pugs and even tame monkeys.

The first decoy recorded in England was built for Sir William Wodehouse at Waxham (Lincolnshire) in 1641, and John Evelyn noted in his Diary that, in 1665, Charles II commissioned a similar decoy 'on a small lake near London', part of which now survives in St James Park. Sydrach Hilcus, a Dutchman, built the decoy and today the small island at the east end of the lake is called Duck Island. In 1670 a similar decoy was built for the Earl of Lincoln on Borough Fen, six miles north of Peterborough.

As drainage of the fens progressed so did the number of decoys increase. At the beginning of the nineteenth century records show that in Essex there were twenty nine working decoys, thirty in Norfolk, twelve in Suffolk, and over forty in Lincolnshire. The most successful decoys were able to catch over 5,000 duck annually, one of the most prolific decoys being that of Holme Fen, near Whittlesey in Cambridgeshire, which was managed by the Skelton family. In 1815 it was not unusual for this decoy to trap thirty dozen duck daily. Just north of Mildenhall at Lakenheath in Suffolk there was another decoy on Sedge Fen. This was worked regularly until 1850 and the decoyman often sent a ton of duck to the London market twice a week.

By the 1950s there were only a handful of working decoys remaining and these included Orwell Park in Suffolk, March House in Essex, Borough Fen in Northants and Fritton Lake, near Lowestoft, where, in 1886, no less than eight pipes were in constant use. Today none remain in East Anglia in working order and the nearest to be found is probably at Boarstall, near Brill in Buckinghamshire, where one pipe is used for trapping duck so that they can be ringed for recording purposes.

Today, a study of large scale maps of a particular district can often give a clue as to where the decoys were once sited. Names like Decoy Fen, Decoy Pond and the Decoy Inn can be reliable clues. One relic that does remain is a law on the Statute Book that forbids 'the discharge of any musket within two miles upwind of a working decoy or half-a-mile downwind' – so all sportsmen have been warned!

A pipe at the Boarstall duck decoy in Buckinghamshire showing the tawny-coloured *'kooikerhondje'* leaping over a hurdle to entice the duck which, when caught, are ringed before being released.

One of the pipes at Fritton duck decoy in 1885. The decoyman has with him his Dutch-bred dog.
(Norfolk Rural Life Museum, Gressenhall)

SIR PETER LELY – 1618 – Cornelis van Tromp –
(1629-1691). *(© National Maritime Museum, London)*

ENGLISH SCHOOL 17th CENTURY – Robert Blake
(1599-1657). General at Sea.
(© National Maritime Museum, London)

WILLIAM Van der VELDE – Calm – HMS ROYAL JAMES – a Royal Yacht.
(© National Maritime Museum, London)

BERCKMAN HENDRICK – Admiral de Ruyter.
(© National Maritime Museum, London)

HOLLAR WENCESLAUS – Engraver – 1647. A Dutch East Indiaman with two ships at anchor.
(© *National Maritime Museum, London*)

Chapter IX

THE ANGLO - DUTCH WARS

The three hard-fought naval wars with the Dutch may now appear as a cruel irrelevancy but in the middle of the seventeenth century the commercial survival of both the warring nations was at stake. The seven United Provinces that comprised the Netherlands had Holland, the most powerful province, as their leader with Amsterdam as its rich capital. The Thirty Years War had enabled Amsterdam to eclipse Antwerp as the new commercial and financial centre; and the British to dominate the Mediterranean trade. The rivalry between the two trading nations grew fiercer as the Dutch gained the ascendancy, and Amsterdam, together with the lesser ports, became entrepôts for goods in transit between the East Indies and Europe.

Dutch *'fluits'* – large, blunt-bowed, three-masted trading vessels – carried smaller crews and were thus more economical than English ships and, by 1650, were carrying 80% of the Spanish wool destined for the flourishing weaving industry both in East Anglia and the Netherlands. English merchants were humiliated by the sight of their imports of wool, wine, timber and tar all arriving in Dutch vessels.

In 1651, Cromwell and the Commonwealth passed the Navigation Act under the terms of which the import of goods in any vessels, other than English, or those of the producer country, was forbidden. In addition, the valuable harvest of herrings, a staple food of the Dutch, could only be exported in English ships. Thus a national monopoly was created which was understandably hotly resented by the Dutch who claimed that 'the flag flown on a vessel covered the cargo carried'. However, the Dutch, despite their rage, desired to remain neutral as any armed conflict could but disrupt trade. But what really riled the Dutch was England's claim to the sovereignty of the seas, with the accompanying demand that all foreign ships must lower their flags in salute to passing English vessels. The Dutch captains had been instructed not to comply, and their refusal had resulted in the seizure of 170 of their merchantmen.

The first Anglo-Dutch war started in May 1652, when a Dutch warship, escorting merchantmen up the Channel, refused to dip its flag, and was therefore promptly fired upon by an English man-of-war. A few weeks later the admirals of the two opposing fleets, Blake and Tromp, clashed off Dover and the war then began in earnest.

The ensuing three wars were unusual in that they were superbly chronicled and illustrated by the Van der Veldes, father and son, whose 'galliot' – a small but sturdy two-masted sailing ship – was present at most of the battles, dodging the shot from both sides. Their ringside view resulted in a series of drawings and paintings which captured the full horror of destructive naval warfare. The young John Constable was so impressed by this work that his first submissions to the Royal Academy were of similar seascapes.

The battles were fought in the shallow waters of the North Sea and the Channel which, never more than 120 feet deep, enabled the warships to drop anchor when winds were unfavourable, and to repair their battered rigging. The Dutch were masters of their indented shoreline with its shifting shoals and channels, and this allowed their ships on several occasions to avoid greater damage as they slipped away under cover of darkness.

Even after the first shots were fired in anger, the Commonwealth was still trying to forge a union with the United Provinces whose one aim was to remain independent. They had only just seen off the Spanish, after a protracted and bloody war, and were suspicious of the more radical Puritanism displayed by the regicides of the Commonwealth; the Dutch Reformed Church was more akin to the Presbyterianism of the Scots who were not anti-royalist. Negotiations foundered, and the only solution appeared to be war.

The first campaign in 1652 started well for the English as the Dutch ships were both undermanned and outgunned. The first engagements off Guernsey and the Kentish Knock shoal, in the summer of 1652, showed up the weakness of the Dutch vessels which were no match for the 100-gun *Sovereign*, and even the second-raters that each mounted sixty guns. Blake, the much respected and experienced English admiral, was instructed to destroy the Dutch merchantmen, and especially those which were laden with valuable spices, pepper, and silks from the East Indies. The Dutch herring fleet of over 600 busses was also a prime target as were the *fluits* carrying wood and pitch from the Baltic, the raw materials needed for the construction of men-of-war. Blake, to his great credit, had no desire to wage war on non-combatants, and all the crews he captured were sent back to their home ports.

After these initial victories, the English rashly dispersed their formidable fleet, thereby underestimating the Dutch determination to repair and replace damaged vessels. Tromp returned in the autumn with a smaller fleet, but this did not deter him from provoking Blake into a series of hard-fought individual actions off Dungeness. These left the depleted English fleet in a sorry state, and powerless to prevent Tromp from sweeping the Channel clear of allied merchantmen; this was when he was supposed to have lashed a broom to his mainmast as an insult to his enemies. He even had the temerity to land crews on Romney marsh in Kent to seize sheep and cattle from the bewildered farmers. Canvey Island was the scene of a similar incursion in 1667.

During the ensuing winter the English licked their wounds, and wisely concentrated on rebuilding the fleet. Crews for the new ships were hard to find and the Commonwealth was forced to improve the working conditions of the sailors: they were to be paid more, and regularly. In addition, the dependants of those killed in action were not forgotten – a remarkably liberal attitude for the times. Press gangs were active in every port and they even targeted the crews of the fleet of Newcastle colliers when they docked in the Thames.

The Dutch tactic in naval warfare was to disable an enemy ship by firing into the rigging, and then overwhelm the crew by armed boarding parties. The ship could then be taken as a prize. Alternately, fireships were floated against it to make it catch fire and blow up. The English, on the other hand, relied on superior gunnery: they poured shot, in controlled broadsides, into the hulls of the enemy with the aim of sinking them. As a way of defeating the Dutch boarding parties, the English embarked regular soldiers, known as Marines, who were also empowered to enforce discipline on board the ships.

In February 1653, Tromp was escorting a fleet of 150 merchant ships up the Channel when he espied the scattered English fleet down wind of him off Portland Bill. He promptly attacked Blake's squadron, one of three into which the fleet was traditionally divided, but Blake was able to withstand the onslaught until Sir William Penn and George Monck, the commanders of the other two squadrons, came to his aid. The ensuing battle proved disastrous for the Dutch who lost seventeen men-of-war, sixteen merchantmen and over 3,000 men killed or captured. It was only Tromp's great skill that averted an even greater disaster.

Many of the captured prisoners were sent to the fens where their compatriot, Cornelius Vermuyden, was busy draining the land and desperate for more labour to dig the dykes and channels.

Later in the same year the English, under Monck, won another battle off the Gabbard, a shoal offshore from Harwich, by adopting a line-ahead formation which depended for its success on a much improved signalling system.

In August, the fiercest engagement yet took place off Scheveningen, when Maarten Tromp was ordered to take his fleet out of Texel in order to raise the English blockade of the Dutch ports. Both fleets suffered greatly; Tromp was killed, and Blake forced to retire to Southwold in Suffolk, to land the wounded and carry out urgent repairs. During the battle the English fleet had used up over 800 tons of shot, and 1,000 barrels of gunpowder – an indication as to how expensive it was to wage such warfare.

The Texel battle marked the end of the first Anglo-Dutch war which was followed by an uneasy peace, negotiated between

Cromwell and the States-General, the body representing the Seven Provinces. The arch-republican, De Wit, made certain that the supporters of the House of Orange, with their overt Royalist sympathies, would never be able to hold the offices of Stadtholder, admiral, or captain-general of the armed forces. This move denied Charles, now exiled in Holland, the chance of grabbing back the English throne with the help of the 'Orangeists'.

The peace treaty was signed in 1654, Cromwell presenting to each of the Dutch envoys a metrical version of Psalm 123, which includes the optimistic verse, "behold how good and how pleasant it is for brethren to dwell together in unity".

Such worthy sentiment was not, alas, to endure after the death of Cromwell in 1658, and the restoration of the monarchy two years later. Charles II had no time for republicans such as those in Holland who controlled the mercantile wealth of the Netherlands, the prime target of English aggression. The Navigation Act was made more onerous by inserting a clause stating that all colonial products had first to be imported before re-export; this restriction was a direct attack on the lucrative Dutch entrepôt trade. Furthermore, foreign factors were to be excluded from the colonies, and three quarters of all ships' crews had to be British. As rivalry between Dutch and English traders along the West African coast, and in the other spheres covered by the two competing East India companies, had already resulted in armed conflict, a new 'casus belli' was not hard to find.

In August 1664, Major Robert Nicolls led an expedition to North America with the object of capturing the Dutch colonies of New Netherlands, and those along the Delaware river. The excuse for this aggression was that the colonists had flouted the Navigation Act. De Ruyter, meanwhile, had been active recapturing the West African trading stations that were first annexed by Sir Robert Holmes earlier in the same year.

Charles II, emboldened by the anti-Dutch sentiments of both Parliament and his close coterie of Cavaliers, sought an excuse to renew hostilities and cripple the Dutch merchant marine. The huge sum of £2,500,000 was voted for the strengthening of the Navy, and the King's brother, the Duke of York, was to command the fleet, flying his flag in the Red squadron. Prince Rupert had the White squadron and Montagu, the Earl of Sandwich, the Blue. The three admirals composed a new set of *'Fighting Instructions'*, which relied upon the men-of-war all keeping in line ahead during an engagement; they were not to seek individual actions.

In March 1665, England declared war on the United Provinces whose leaders, expecting this move, had not been idle during the short period of peace. They had built up a fleet of over one hundred ships, some carrying sixty or more guns. To quell bitter rivalries over the command of this formidable fleet, it was divided into seven squadrons under the Lord of Obdan, with Cornelis Tromp, son of the great admiral, and De Wit, as his assistants.

The first test for the re-assembled fleets was in June 1665, when they clashed off Lowestoft. The English were favoured by a south-west wind which carried the sound of the guns as far inland as London. Obdan's flagship soon caught fire and blew up, killing him and 400 of his crew. This was the signal for the Dutch to withdraw and head for the safe havens of the Maas estuary and Texel. The Dutch losses numbered over 5,000 which included three flag officers; the English lost only one merchantmen but far more serious was the loss of three admirals and two senior captains. This probably explained why a golden opportunity was missed of pursuing and destroying the entire Dutch fleet. After the battle, the victors dispersed to celebrate in havens between Harwich and Chatham; they should have been blockading the Dutch ports.

De Ruyter had meanwhile been protecting a fleet of East Indiamen which, having taken shelter in the port of Bergen op Zoom, were on the last leg of their long voyage home. A fierce gale scattered the convoy and two ships were captured and sailed to London as valuable prizes. Samuel Pepys records in his Diary how the cabins and holds were stuffed with peppers, cloves, nutmegs, copperplate and bales of exotic silks.

Once again the Dutch fleet was rapidly repaired, and soon

made its presence felt by blockading the Thames estuary. It was only the imminent onset of the plague, already rife in London, that caused the Dutch to retire.

The English by now had little money left for much-needed repairs. They had to face the double threat posed by the Dutch and the French, who had declared war on Britain in January 1666. In June of that year the opposing fleets engaged in running battles while Prince Rupert's squadron chased the elusive French fleet. After three days of fighting, Monck only had forty serviceable ships, half the number available to the Dutch, and was only saved when Prince Rupert returned from his fruitless chase. The English lost the *Royal Prince*, burnt by a Dutch fire-ship, and two admirals; Admiral Ayscue, the senior admiral, was captured and ended up as a prisoner in the castle of Loevenstein.

A few weeks later, on St James Day, July 25th, the fleets clashed off Orford Ness on the Suffolk coast. Superior English firepower forced Cornelis Tromp to retire, closely pursued by the English who, with the help of a disaffected Dutch ship's captain, invaded the islands of Vlieland and Terschelling, where storehouses were destroyed and more than 150 merchantmen burnt at their moorings.

De Wit's furious response to this daring raid was to mount a similar incursion on the English mainland. He scoured the prisons for sailors who could pilot his vessels up the Thames estuary; a Colonel Dolman, an English soldier with strong republican sympathies, was chosen for this work. The invasion fleet was commanded by De Ruyter who embarked a recently formed marine corps and put Dolman in charge of it.

The Dutch blockaded the mouth of the Thames, and then sent seventeen small vessels with raiding parties aboard, and fireships up the Medway with instructions to destroy as many warships as possible. The surprised English were slow to react. Sheerness Fort was quickly captured, and the chain, with its attendant guardships, across the Medway at Gillingham proved no obstacle. The capital ships moored beyond were easy prey and six of the largest were burnt. The majestic *Prince Charles* was refloated and sailed away by the triumphant Dutch sailors. This humiliating display of the enemy's maritime power on London's doorstep forced Charles to sue for peace, while De Wit was crowned with the laurels of a victor.

Charles was left with little room for manoeuvre; he was desperately short of money, and Dutch depredations had halved the revenue from customs duties. Louis XIV seized the opportunity to bribe Charles with cash, in return for English support for an invasion of the Netherlands, and for a promise to withdraw constraints on Catholics and 'other non-conformists'. Charles even offered to make England a Catholic country under the terms of the secret Treaty of Dover.

The French proceeded to invade the United Provinces whose only sure defence was to flood the polders that had been so painstakingly reclaimed from the sea. The English undertook to destroy the Dutch fleet so that the French could also launch an invasion from the sea. Thus began the third and final Anglo-Dutch war.

At dawn, on May 28th 1672, De Ruyter bore down from the north-east to engage the English and French fleets, numbering seventy one ships, that were strung out along the east coast from Aldeburgh to Southwold. Many of the crews were still ashore. The dreaded fireships spearheaded the attack, and the squadron commanded by the Earl of Sandwich soon found itself in the thick of the fighting. The admiral's flagship of 100 guns – the *Royal James* – was isolated, rammed, and set on fire. Sandwich was drowned and his body, recognisable by the Garter Ribbon he had been wearing, was discovered ten days later by a salvage crew searching for lost anchors. The attack and destruction of the *Royal James* was the subject of a famous painting by the Van der Veldes; the same scene is portrayed on a stained glass window at Hinchinbrooke House at Huntingdon where the unfortunate Earl once lived.

The battle raged throughout the day in Sole Bay, within plain view of the watchers who lined the nearby shore. Later that night a gale blew up, a fog rolled in and the same watchers had the sad task of receiving over 800 wounded sailors, and retrieving hundreds of corpses from the beaches. The Dutch had lost two of their largest warships but had savaged an enemy fleet by dint of superior tactics and sterner discipline. The French fleet, both in this and previous encounters, had stood off and played little part in the battles.

There were two further attempts, in 1673, to lure the Dutch warships out of their harbours, and these resulted in inconclusive battles at Schooneveld off Texel. While the Dutch fleet remained intact, the French could not invade so there was a stalemate. The young Stadtholder, the future William III of Britain, sensing that the English were now heartily tired of war, and disenchanted with their French allies, agreed to sign the Treaty of Westminster in 1674 by which the English retained their sovereignty of the 'Narrow Seas'. The decks were now cleared for the long war against the Catholic 'Sun King', Louis XIV, and the continuing supremacy of the English navy owed much to the lessons from fighting the Dutch during the preceding three wars.

Chapter X

PICTURES and PAINTINGS

The small village of Worstead, north of Norwich, can claim more affinity with the Netherlands than almost any other in Norfolk. It gave its name to the fine woven cloth for which the whole area became famous, and many of its houses display an unmistakable Flemish influence. And at the centre of the village is the parish church of St Mary, built in the 1380s, with a commanding tower over 100ft high. The chancel, in Decorated style, retains the original rood screen of 1512 with its sixteen panels, attributed to six different artists, which were inspired by or even copied from contemporary Flemish engravings of the Apostles and the Saints. St Peter the Apostle is as Lucas van Leyden portrayed him and another St Peter is as originally engraved by Martin Schongauer. It is marvellous that, despite the iconoclasm of the Reformation and the Commonwealth, these panels survive, their colours expertly restored to their original brilliance.

In the great 'Marshland' churches between Wisbech and King's Lynn are other Flemish masterpieces, their survival due to the pro-Commonwealth sympathies of the parishioners who kept Dowsing and his henchmen away from their revered places of worship. In Terrington St Clements the church font has a cover decorated with seventeenth century paintings by a Flemish artist showing scenes from the life of Jesus, and at Terrington St John the Baptist there is a beautiful carving of the angel Gabriel (or perhaps of the Virgin Mary?) by an unknown fifteenth century craftsman.

The Flemish in the sixteenth century were renowned for their portrayal of religious subjects through the media of paint and engraving. Their altarpieces with two or more folding panels graced many East Anglian churches. One such triptych was commissioned in

1520 by a scion of a Norfolk family, the Knyvetts, for their parish church at Ashwellthorpe, south of Norwich. The subject chosen was the 'Seven Sorrows of the Virgin Mary', portrayed in the form of a visual pilgrimage through a landscape. This wonderful example of Flemish art is now preserved at Norwich Castle Museum. Another larger and beautifully restored Flemish altarpiece of c.1510 can be seen in the Bedingfeld family chapel in the grounds of Oxburgh Hall in south-west Norfolk.

In the seventeenth century, just across the 'German Ocean', the markets and art galleries were full of the works of Netherlandish artists who were becoming increasingly drawn towards the painting of *'landschapps';* it was the Dutch who gave us the word 'landscapes' and also demonstrated their skills in painting them. It helped that the burgeoning prosperity in the Low Countries created an affluent merchant class which could afford to buy these paintings.

East Anglia and the Netherlands share an intimacy with the sea, the wide openness of their skies, and the clouds that sail across them like galleons driven before great winds. Because the shared scenery on land was often unspectacular, the artist could concentrate on the subtle interplay between colour, tone and space. These influences helped the Dutch to become the pioneers of landscape painting in Europe and who inspired the English artists of the stature of Crome, Constable and Cotman.

Thomas Gainsborough, born at Sudbury in 1727, was inspired first by his own Suffolk countryside and then by the major works of the Dutch masters. He once claimed that 'there was not a picturesque clump of trees, nor a single tree of any beauty, no, nor hedgerow, stem or post in the district' that was not firmly fixed in his memory. During his 'Suffolk' period before moving to Bath and thence to London, his subjects were all close to nature, and drawn in pencil or black chalk on white paper, a technique that later had a strong influence on the work of artists of the Norwich School such as John Crome.

Crome was born in 1768, the son of a journeyman weaver and landlord of the Griffin Inn in Norwich. Having first taught himself how to read and write he became an errand boy to a local physician, Dr Rigby, in whose employ he made useful contacts. When fifteen, he was apprenticed to a coach and sign painter for seven years which enabled him to earn a living and learn a trade. From an early age he was determined to be an artist and so took every opportunity to study the work of established artists, and observe the natural world around him. He was fortunate to have been noticed by a wealthy master-weaver, Thomas Harvey of Catton, near Norwich, whose wife came from Rotterdam. Crome could also have known Jeremiah Ives of Catton Hall for whom Humphry Repton had executed his first landscape commission in 1788. Harvey owned a valuable collection of paintings that included works by Richard Wilson and Gainsborough, as well as by Meindert Hobbema who was once apprenticed to Ruysdael in Amsterdam. Hobbema's landscapes were particularly admired by the British and we know that his picture 'The Road Side Inn' much impressed Crome as did works by Jan Wijnants and Jan van Goyen. The story goes that when Crome was on his death bed in 1821 his last words were 'Oh, Hobbema, my dear Hobbema, how I have loved you!'

Crome painted his first landscape in 1786 and by 1806 he was able to produce such exquisite works as 'The Yare at Thorpe'. His technique was to prepare a ground of cream which was then covered by a pinkish priming coat very similar to the preparation adopted by the Dutch landscape painters. He also used a paint brush handle when painting trees, a trick usually associated with Rembrandt.

The only time Crome travelled abroad was in 1814 to visit the Louvre in Paris where the important pictures acquired by Napoleon during his campaign had been assembled. It was very likely that en route home to Norfolk he passed through the Netherlands and took the opportunity of viewing the works of Flemish and Dutch masters.

It was Crome who provided the impetus for the founding of the Norwich Society in 1803, later to become the Norwich Society of Artists or the 'Norwich School'. He exhibited at the Society's first exhibition in 1805 and was elected President in 1808. James Stark, a pupil of Crome and a leading Member of the Society, was forthright in attributing much of his success to the skills exhibited by the Dutch painters. John Bright, another leading Society Member, excelled in painting dramatic, stormy skies that were direct reflections of works by Rembrandt and Ruysdael.

Emily Stannard was another Society Member who owed much to the Dutch masters of still life painting such as Van Huysum and Jan Brueghel whose works she was able to study during a visit to Holland with her father in 1820. She became expert at portraying dead game, and a study of a hare and a pheasant, dated 1853, is very similar to a painting of 1706 by Jan Weenix in the Fitzwilliam Museum.

The other great East Anglian artist, John Constable, was more than any other a product of his native countryside. He was born in 1776 at East Bergholt in Suffolk where his father owned watermills on the River Stour in a valley that would inspire so many of Constable's finest landscapes. By the age of seventeen Constable had determined to be a painter and was fortunate enough in 1775 to be noticed by J.T. Smith who became Keeper of prints and drawings at the British Museum. Four years later he was admitted as a student to the Royal Academy and occupied himself with copying the landscape paintings of such masters as Ruysdael, Wilson and Gainsborough. The Dutch marine artists such as the Van der Veldes also influenced Constable; one of the first watercolours he exhibited at the Royal Academy was a study of *HMS Victory* during the battle of Trafalgar.

But his fame stems from his ideal of a natural style of landscape painting, epitomised both by '*The Hay Wain*', a canvas unveiled at the Louvre in 1824, and the effect which his revolutionary style had on the European landscape painters who were to follow him.

Sir Joshua Reynolds, perhaps the most distinguished of all English portrait painters, summed it up in 1784 when he told his students 'painters should go to the Dutch school to learn the Art of

Painting, just as they would go to a grammar school to learn languages'. And to study and admire the art of the Netherlands there is nowhere better to do this in East Anglia than the Fitzwilliam Museum in Cambridge whose collection includes no less than 164 Dutch and Flemish paintings, and a number of drawings by Rembrandt. The Decorative arts are also well represented; the Glaisher Bequest of Delftware comprises over 500 pieces and there are many valuable books, manuscripts, medals and coins of Dutch and Flemish provenance.

Such a wealth of exhibits is not surprising when one realises that the three families through whose generosity the Museum was so well endowed all had their roots either in Flanders or Holland.

The Founder, Richard, 7th Viscount Fitzwilliam, owed his fortune to his mother, Catherine, who was the daughter of Sir Mathew Decker, a Flemish merchant as well as an astute financier, one of many who followed William and Mary to England in 1688. He soon gained favour with the political leaders whose main task at that time was to finance the King's constant campaigning against the French and Spanish. His close connections with the wealthy Dutch merchants and his role as leader of the immigrant communities in London, centred on their church of Austin Friars, soon made him very rich. He bought a house in St James Square, where he was surrounded by the most influential members of the aristocracy. He also owned a house at Richmond on the Thames which had a greenhouse for the cultivation of pineappples – an achievement recorded for posterity by the painter Netscher in 1716 on the occasion of the presentation to George I of one of the first fruits.

He became a discerning collector of art and was advised by such experts as Sir Andrew Fountaine of Narford Hall in Norfolk. When he died in 1749 he bequeathed his estate to his widow who, in turn, passed it on to her daughter, Catherine, who married the 6th Viscount Fitzwilliam. It was their son, Richard, who inherited the title and the Decker fortune which enabled him to found the Museum which was opened in 1816.

The second family of benefactors were Protestant silkweavers from Flanders who were forced to emigrate after the Revocation of the Edict of Nantes in 1685. Their name was Mesman and they settled first in Canterbury before moving to Spitalfields in east London to join the many other Huguenot weavers who were allowed to settle there and carry on their trade outside the City walls. The Mesmans prospered and when Daniel died in 1834 he bequeathed his collection of 300 paintings to the Fitzwilliam.

The Van Sittart family, in the person of Arthur Van Sittart, gave to the Museum between 1852 and 1880 some outstanding works of art, including paintings by Hobbema, Ruysdael and Adrian Van der Velde. His Dutch ancestors came over to England from Limburg in c.1670 and each generation of the family excelled in various walks of life; Arthur's great-uncle was a Chancellor of the Exchequer and his father a general.

The Fitzwilliam, therefore, is a powerful reminder of the vital Anglo-Netherlands connection; the exhibits on show are constantly changing and entry is free.

Other examples of Netherlandish art can be admired in the collections of paintings in the great country houses of East Anglia. The Grand Tour was recommended as an excellent way for young gentlemen from landed families to gain experience of other cultures and a taste for the arts. Accompanied by tutors and cicerones, the youths followed well-recognised routes through France to Italy. Their return journey was via the Tyrol, Germany and the Netherlands; Rotterdam being the usual port of embarkation for England. The Tour became so popular that, then as now, the 'tourists' complained of the impossibility of escaping from their fellow countrymen.

The works of art and mementoes acquired by the 'tourists' laid the foundations for many of the fine collections that we can enjoy today. The first of Norfolk's young gentlemen 'tourists' was Ashe Windham of Felbrigg Hall in Norfolk. He travelled between 1693 and 1696 in the company of a cicerone, one Patrick St Clair, who knew Holland well from previous visits. Windham was so enthused by his travels that he sent his son, William II, to Europe in 1738 with Benjamin Stillingfleet, the original 'bluestocking' intellectual, as his tutor.

They returned through Holland in 1742 and the choicest pictures brought back with them are displayed in the Cabinet at Felbrigg, a lasting tribute to a gentleman whose taste was cultivated by the Grand Tour. In particular, Windham admired the Dutch marine artists and bought six canvasses by the Van der Veldes, and another by Simon de Vlieger, painted in 1630, depicting the blockade of Amoy by the Dutch fleet; this masterpiece still hangs in its original place on one wall of the Cabinet.

Hard on Windham's heels were the young Walpoles from Houghton Hall, including George who was to become the 3ʳᵈ Earl of Orford and vilified for selling the cream of the great Walpole picture collection to Catherine the Great of Russia in 1769. Among the pictures sold were thirteen renowned works by Rembrandt, four by Snyders and another four by van Dyck. Most of these can be seen at the Hermitage in St Petersburg.

Charles Townshend, 3ʳᵈ Viscount and the owner of Raynham Hall in Norfolk, sent his second son, also Charles, to study Law at Leiden University and encouraged him to travel in the Netherlands in order to broaden his education. The family thus acquired several fine paintings, one of which by Hondercoeter was lent in 1829 to an exhibition of Old Masters held in Norwich.

Not all the 'tourists', however, were from the great families. There was, for example, James Coldham from King's Lynn who set off for Holland in 1754 to improve his languages, especially French, and to learn about classical art and architecture. He sailed from Wells-next-the-Sea for Rotterdam and finished his Tour in Brussels where he was very impressed 'by pieces... by Rembrandt and Vandyke and landskips by Teniers and some few by Poussin'. He also commented on 'ye general neatness which prevails throughout all Holland'. It is known that he brought back with him prints of works by Teniers and Raphael.

In Holkham Hall, in Norfolk, can be appreciated an example of what is probably the most imposing legacy of the Grand Tour anywhere in England, and a family's passion for collecting classical art and sculpture. Thomas Coke, the 1st Earl of Leicester, who had spent no less than five and a half years as a minor travelling abroad, amassed a superb collection of manuscripts, statuary and pictures to house which he built Holkham in grand, Palladian style. His great-nephew, Thomas William Coke, added to the collection which contains several Netherlandish masterpieces, notably *'The Return of the Holy Family'* by Rubens, a portrait of the *'Duc d' Arenberg on Horseback'* by Van Dyck – purchased in Paris in 1718 – and two allegorical paintings of birds by Hondercoeter. There are also classical landscapes by Jan Frans Van Bloemen who moved to Rome in 1681 and changed his name to Orizzonte.

Mathew Brettingham junior, the young architect and designer who had helped Thomas Coke both to build Holkham and assemble his great art collection, was commissioned by the 2nd Duke of Grafton to re-model Euston Hall, near Bury St Edmunds. The estate was originally purchased in 1666 in a ruinous condition by Henry Bennet, Earl of Arlington, who married Isabella van Beverwaert, the grand-daughter of Maurice, Prince of Orange. He joined Charles II in exile in 1654 and, after the Restoration, served as Secretary of State in the famous CABAL government. Through these strong Royal Stuart connections the Grafton family at Euston was able to acquire a marvellous collection of portraits of the Stuarts by Van Dyck and Sir Peter Lely. Of great historical interest is a painting, near the top of the main staircase, of the great ball held at the Hague the night before Charles II returned to Britain to claim his throne. He is seen dancing with his sister, the Princess of Orange.

Just as the wealthy merchants of the Low Countries were able to afford to collect the pictures of their native artists in the seventeenth century, so in the next century could the new and affluent British merchant class create their own collections. The upheaval in Europe caused by the French Revolution resulted in a flood of paintings on to the art market, and many of these new collectors were thus able to acquire paintings at affordable prices. So just when the 'Norwich School' was about to establish itself there were many private collections of quality to which its members could have had access. And in these collections the Netherlandish masters would have been very well represented. As the fortunes of the amateur collectors waned so their pictures were dispersed but it is fortunate indeed that a fair proportion of them have ended up in the Castle Museum in Norwich and other municipal galleries in East Anglia.

UNKNOWN - Portrait of Sir Mathew Decker. *(© Fitzwilliam Museum, Cambridge)*

WILLEM Van der VELDE – Battle of the Texel – Fought in 1673 between the combined English and French fleets, and the Dutch fleet under the command of de Ruyter.
(© National Trust Photographic Library/John Hammond –The Windham Collection)

Sir PETER PAUL RUBENS – The Return of the Holy Family – *(© Lord Leicester and Trustees of the Holkham Estate)*

MEINDERT HOBBEMA – Wooded landscape with a hawking party – c.1667.
(© Fitzwilliam Museum, Cambridge)

JAN WEENIX – Flowers and Fruit in a landscape.
(© Fitzwilliam Museum, Cambridge)

EMILY STANNARD (nee EMILY
COPPIN) – Still Life – Dead Ducks and
a Hare with Basket and a Sprig
of Holly – 1853.
(© Norwich Castle Museum and Art Gallery)

WORSTEAD CHURCH – The rood screen of 1512 with 16 panels depicting Saints and Apostles.

JOHN CROME – The River Yare at Thorpe, Norwich – c.1806. (© *Norwich Castle Museum and Art Gallery*)

JAN DAVIDSZ de HEEM – Flower-piece – c.1660. (© *Fitzwilliam Museum, Cambridge*)

MELCHIOR HONDERCOETER – Emblematic representations of King William's wars.
(© *Lord Leicester and Trustees of the Holkham Estate*)

The Peterson Cup in the form of a tazza or standing dish. A smaller cup, given to the city of Norwich in 1574 by Peter Peterson the Dutch goldsmith, was melted down and more silver added in order to make the present cup that bears the mark of Cobbold and the date 1580. *(By kind permission of Norwich City Council)*

A pair of tulip vases and other Delftware pottery made by Adriaen Kocks who acquired the Greek A pottery on the Thames in 1686. He supplied these items to Sir William Blathwayt at Dyrham Park, near Bath, who was then Secretary of State to William III. *(The Blathwayt Collection, the National Trust – photo: Christopher Hurst)*

The Howard Basin, embossed with scenes of the Triumph of Neptune, dated 1617-18, and probably made for Thomas, Earl of Arundel, adviser on art to Charles I, by a Dutch goldsmith. *(By kind permission of Norwich City Council)*

A rare Delft dish made in 1696 from clay which would have come either from Tournai in Flanders or from Mulheim in Germany. *(Private collection)*

Chapter XI

CUPS, POTS AND CLOCKS

Mention pottery, and the word *Delft* immediately springs to mind, because it is a generic name, derived from the eponymous town in Holland, for one of the most ancient processes for making pots. Known also as faience or majolica, Delftware is pottery glazed with tin oxide, a method that the Babylonians used in c.1000 BC .

In the eighth century AD Persian potters rediscovered and refined the Babylonian process, which was then taken up by the Arabs, some of whom introduced it to North Africa. In 711 AD the Moors succesfully invaded the Iberian peninsula, using Mallorca in the Balearic islands as a stepping stone, hence the name *majolica* for the pottery that went with them.

Over the years the Moorish glazed pottery spread through France and Italy before finally reaching Delft where the raw materials were readily available for pottery manufacture. Wherever suitable clay is found, it should be possible to throw Delft pots, a fact known by two enterprising potters from Antwerp who, in 1567, petitioned Queen Elizabeth to be allowed to settle in Norwich; their names were Jasper Andries and Jacob Janson, Protestant refugees from religious persecution.

They discovered that the clay found along the banks of the river Yare in Norfolk was ideal for Delftware, and that they could obtain tin from the mines in Cornwall. The metal was oxidised at the pottery, and then fused with lead and glass. Cobalt oxide gave the blue coloration while green was obtained from copper. Other shades were purple from manganese, brick red from iron, and yellow from antimony. All these colour compounds were chosen as they could withstand the high temperatures required for firing the pots.

By 1571 the Flemish potters had moved to London, using the clay found along the banks of the river Thames. They were followed by many more Dutch and Flemish craftsmen who continued to produce Delftware which was much in demand both locally and in northern Europe.

The refugees also brought with them their own tin glazed pots and cooking vessels; these included decorated jugs and earthenware frying pans, fine samples of which are displayed at the Castle Museum in Norwich. The modern non-stick frying pan can perhaps be traced back to the Flemish exiles who settled in Norwich?

The best known product of the Delft potteries is the square, glazed tile, usually decorated with crudely painted rural scenes and watery landscapes. The tiles were used most often to decorate fireplaces, but could also be fitted together to create whole pictures within a colourful border. Wonderful examples of these framed tiles can be seen at the Stedelijk Museum in Leiden.

The English Delft potteries sited beside the Thames were able to produce elegant, polychrome ware which now grace several collections in Norfolk – at Houghton Hall in particular. In the Castle Museum is a Delft bottle from the Lambeth pottery, inscribed with the initials *E.M.W.* and the date, *1649,* together with the arms of the Grocers Company. This inscription refers to a wealthy Norwich grocer called E.M.Woodward.

At the end of the seventeenth century there was a brisk trade in items bearing crude portraits of William III and his Queen, Mary II. The owners of these pots would be seen to be staunch Royalists; it mattered little that the portraits bore only a passing resemblance to the Royal couple. There are many examples of pottery of this period in the comprehensive Glaisher Collection of Delftware at the Fitzwilliam Museum in Cambridge.

The influx of the Dutch and Flemish Strangers to Norwich helped to make the city the wealthiest in the kingdom, after London and Bristol. Among these immigrants were several goldsmiths, many of whose names are known thanks to the introduction of Norwich's own assay mark in 1565. In that year Peter Peterson I was registered as Warden of the Goldsmiths Company; he was again elected Warden in 1570 together with 'Dutch George' Fenne who became a freeman by purchase in 1567, as well as a leading Elder of the Dutch Church in Norwich.

There was plenty of work to occupy the goldsmiths as all the parish churches in Norfolk, and many in Suffolk, were ordered to use the new communion cups and pattens as required by the Reformation of 1547. Peterson avoided becoming Sheriff of Norwich by presenting to the city a silver cup which was later melted down; William Cobbold used the metal to make a valuable tazza. This impressive example of Cobbold's skill, weighing thirty two ounces, is now known as the Peterson or Ranson Cup and is in the collection of Norwich's civic plate now on display in the Castle Museum. Also in the collection are a matching basin and ewer, dated 1617-18, embossed with scenes of the triumphs of Neptune and called the Howard Jug, the work of an unknown Dutch goldsmith. The jug was commissioned by the Earl of Arundel who was once the adviser on art to Charles I. Another fine example of the goldsmith's art is a slim, tall flagon, assayed in Norwich in 1631 and presented to the city by a rich Dutch merchant named Tobias De Hem.

With the goldsmiths came the watchmakers and jewellers, all of whom prospered greatly during the period after 1650. One such craftsman was the freeman Johannes Gaskoyne, an exile from the Spanish Netherlands and a devout Calvinist. An earlier arrival was Jacques van Barton whose father had escaped from Brabant with his wife and family in 1567. Jacques became a freeman in 1600, and later commanded the 'Companie of the Militia of Dutch church Members'.

A watchmaker who became famous was a member of the Fromanteel family; originally refugees from Flanders. Born in 1607 in Norwich, Ahasuerus Fromanteel moved to London in 1629 where he was eventually elected a freeman of the Blacksmiths Company and became a founder member of the Company of Watchmakers. He was reputed to have introduced the pendulum into England, and a three-train table clock made by another member of this gifted family, Johannes from Amsterdam, can be admired in the John Gershwin Parkington Memorial collection of time measurement instruments at Bury St Edmunds in Suffolk.

Queen Elizabeth's visit to Norwich in August, 1578, was a memorable occasion. A series of pageants was staged to welcome her; the first portrayed the 'artizans strangers' and told of their industry which contributed so much to the increasing prosperity of the city. Later during her visit the minister of the Dutch church, Hermanus Modet, presented her with a silver gilt cup in a green velvet case on behalf of the foreigh congregations. The Queen in return gave £30 to be distributed among the poorest of the Strangers.

What happened in Norwich was not an isolated affair; time and again the Strangers in many parts of the region were praised for bringing much trade and for making a variety of items that before were unknown. In addition, they provided employment and training for the local populace. No wonder, therefore, that the Catholic monarchs realised only too late how their own economies were suffering from the enforced exodus of so many skilled artisans and craftsmen. The French in particular, at the beginning of the eighteenth century, were saying to the emigrants 'come home, all is forgiven' – but it was too late.

A MAP OF THE NETHERLANDS

The Low Countries – as the boundaries would have appeared in c.1650. The dark line
depicting the frontier of the United Netherlands follows closely the boundary of the Holy
Roman Empire as established by Charlemagne in 800 AD when
Pope Leo III crowned him as Emperor of the West.

WILLIAM III

An ivory medallion portrait of c.1690 by Jean Cavalier, a Huguenot exile who was described as medallist to William III.

For almost six hundred years the Orange-Nassau dynasty has played a leading role in Dutch public life as military commanders, stadholders, political leaders and, finally, as constitutional monarchs. The name of Nassau derives from a twelfth century castle built in the region that now forms part of the German *land* of Hesse. The Nassau family's links with the Netherlands date from 1403 when Count Englebert I of Nassau married Johanna van Polanen, a wealthy Dutch heiress, and then settled in Breda in the Duchy of Brabant.

A descendant, Rene de Chalon, inherited both the Nassau lands in the Low Countries and the autonomous principality of Orange and, on his death in 1544, the principality passed to his cousin, William of Nassau, who later distinguished himself as William of Orange and a founder of the Dutch state.

His name lives on in the Dutch national anthem, the *Wilhelmus*, and the colour orange came to symbolise the Netherlands.

Prince William III married Mary Stuart, eldest daughter of James II, and in 1689 they were jointly crowned as King and Queen of Great Britain. Under William's leadership as King and stadholder, Britain and the Republic of the Netherlands formed the core of a European alliance that was pledged to thwart the expansionist arms of France.

ORANGERY

An engraving of the orangery erected by Magdalena POULLE, mistress of Gunterstein, in the 1680's. The open-air courtyard in front, sheltered by a high, wooden fence, was where the plants were set out in pots during the summer months. An inventory made in August, 1699, of the plants in the orangery included orange, lime, myrtle, jasmine, camphor and double oleander as well as many rare foreign plants.

It is recorded that visitors to Gunterstein were offered candied orange-blossom in a chamber decorated with fragrant garlands of small, green oranges.

SELECTED BIBLIOGRAPHY

BIRD, Yvonne and Clifford – Norfolk and Norwich Clocks and Clockmakers. Phillimore. 1996.

BROWN, R.J. – Windmills of England – Robert Hale, 1979.

CENTRE OF EAST ANGLIAN STUDIES – The Ocean's Gift. 1995.

DOBBS, R.C. – Bulbs in Britain – A Century of Growing – Abbey Printers, –1983.

EBBAGE, Sheridan – Barns and Granaries – Boydell Press, 1976.

ERNLE, Lord. – English Farming, Past and Present – Longmans Green, 1936.

FITZWILLIAM MUSEUM – The Dutch Connection – 1998.

HAINSWORTH, Roger and CHURCHES, Christine – The Anglo-Dutch Naval Wars, 1652-1674. – Sutton Publishing, 1998.

HALEY, K.H.D. – The British and the Dutch – George Philip, 1988.

JARVIS, Stan – Smuggling in East Anglia – Countryside Books, 1987.

JOHNSTON, Andrew – The Protestant Reformation in Europe – Longman, 1996

MOORE, Andrew – Norfolk and the Grand Tour. The Norwich School of Artists. Norfolk Museums Service. 1985.

MURRAY, John – William Bentinck and William III – Grew, 1924.

PASSMORE, J.B. – The English Plough – OUP, 1930.

ROBERTSON-SCOTT, J.W. – War Time and Peace in Holland – Heinemann, 1914.

THOMAS, Graham – Trees in the Landscape – John Murray, 1983.

TICE, Frank – Tales of the East Coast – Watkins Studios, 1995.

WADE-MARTINS, Susannah – 'Turnip' Townshend – Poppyland Publishing, 1990.

WENTWORTH-DAY, J. – History of the Fens – George Harrap, 1973.

WILSON, Charles – Holland and Britain – Collins, 1947.

WINCHESTER, Barbara – Tudor Family Portrait – Jonathan Cape, 1955.

WREN, Wilfrid. J. – Ports of the Eastern Counties – Terence Dalton, 1976.